Issues in Privatizing
Social Security

Issues in Privatizing
Social Security

edited by
Peter A. Diamond

Report of an Expert Panel
of the
National Academy of
Social Insurance

The MIT Press
Cambridge, Massachusetts
London, England

© 1999 National Academy of Social Insurance

Library of Congress Cataloging-in-Publication Data

National Academy of Social Insurance (U.S.). Panel on Privatization
   of Social Security.
      Issues in privatizing Social Security : report of an expert panel
   of the National Academy of Social Insurance / edited by Peter A.
   Diamond.
            p.   cm.
      "The findings and recommendations ... are those of the Panel on
   Privatization of Social Security."—P.   .
      Includes bibliographical references.
      ISBN 0-262-04177-4 (hardcover : alk. paper)
      1. Social Security—United States.   2. Privatization—United
   States.   I. Diamond, Peter A.   II. Title.
   HD7125.N283   1999
   368.4'3'00973—dc21   99-19902
                                                               CIP

National Academy of Social Insurance

The National Academy of Social Insurance is a nonprofit, nonpartisan organization made up of the nation's leading experts on social insurance. Its mission is to conduct research and enhance public understanding of social insurance, to develop new leaders and to provide a nonpartisan forum for exchange of ideas on important issues in the field of social insurance. Social insurance, both in the United States and abroad, encompasses broad-based systems for insuring workers and their families against economic insecurity caused by loss of income from work and protecting individuals against the cost of personal health care services. The Academy's research covers social insurance systems, such as Social Security, Medicare, workers' compensation and unemployment insurance, and related social assistance and private employee benefits.

The Academy convenes study panels that are charged with conducting research, issuing findings and, in some cases, reaching recommendations based on their analyses. Panel members are selected for their recognized expertise and with due consideration for the balance of disciplines and perspectives appropriate to the project. The findings and any recommendations remain those of study panels and do not represent an official position of the Academy or its funders.

In accordance with procedures of the Academy, study panel reports are reviewed by a committee of the Board for completeness, accuracy, clarity and objectivity. The findings and recommendations in this report are those of the Panel on Privatization of Social Security.

The project received financial support from the Alfred P. Sloan Foundation, the AARP Andrus Foundation, TIAA-CREF, and The Actuarial Foundation and in-kind research support from TIAA-CREF.

Panel on Privatization of Social Security Participants
June 1998–November 1998

Peter A. Diamond, Chair
Institute Professor
Massachusetts Institute of
Technology

R. Douglas Arnold (joined 1/97)
William Church Osborn
Professor of Public Affairs
Woodrow Wilson School of Public
and International Affairs
Princeton University

B. Douglas Bernheim
Lewis and Virginia Eaton Professor
Department of Economics
Stanford University

Michael J. Boskin (resigned,
10/98)**
Tully M. Friedman Professor of
Economics, and Senior Fellow,
Hoover Institution
Stanford University

Gary Burtless
Senior Fellow
Economic Studies Program
The Brookings Institution

Yuan Chang
Chairman and CEO (Retired)
Greater China Operations
Metropolitan Life Insurance
Company

Mary C. Daly
Economist
Research Department
Federal Reserve Bank of San
Francisco

Martha Derthick (resigned, 1/97)
Julia Allen Cooper Professor of
Government and Foreign Affairs
University of Virginia

John Geanakoplos
James Tobin Professor of
Economics, and Director, The
Cowles Foundation for Research in
Economics
Yale University

Stephen C. Goss*
Deputy Chief Actuary
Long Range Actuarial Estimates
Social Security Administration

Daniel Halperin
Stanley S. Surrey Professor
Harvard Law School

Hugh Heclo
Clarence J. Robinson Professor of
Public Affairs
George Mason University

* See Statement of Participation, Appendix A.
** See Statement, Appendix B.

Abstract

This study analyzes issues related to two types of Social Security proposals. One type would keep the current Social Security defined-benefit structure, but build and maintain a larger trust fund and invest part of it in stocks and corporate bonds. The other would set up funded individual Social Security accounts, also partially invested in private markets. Both types of proposal would increase advance funding for Social Security, by which we mean raising taxes or lowering benefits in the near term in order to build up and maintain more funds to pay future benefits.

Should Social Security have more advance funding? Advance funding improves the long-run financial status of Social Security, permitting lower taxes and/or higher benefits in the future. Advance funding can add to national savings, which contributes to economic growth, but at a cost of decreased consumption. Advance funding improves money's worth for workers in the future, where money's worth is measured as the rate of return for a cohort of workers on its lifetime Social Security taxes. But the higher returns for future workers come at the expense of lower money's worth for those workers in the near term who pay higher taxes or receive lower benefits in order to increase advance funding. These effects are present with or without individual accounts. The Panel recommends increased advance funding but members differ on whether it is better with or without individual accounts.

Should Social Security funds be invested in the stock market? The Panel concludes that, including consideration of risk, a reformed system would get better long-term returns with a diversified portfolio that includes stocks, but members differ on whether this is better with or without individual accounts. If investments are organized by the government (for the Trust Fund or for individual accounts), independent institutions would be needed to try to shield portfolio decisions and corporate governance from political pressures. A governance institution is proposed modeled after the federal employees' Thrift Savings Plan. If investments are privately organized, a regulatory structure is needed.

Returns on particular Social Security investments (such as in the stock market) should not be confused with money's worth, the return on all of Social Security taxes, some of which go into investments and much of which go to pay for benefits to current retirees and to provide disability benefits and survivors insurance to young families. In addition, in considering the well-being of workers, it is necessary to go beyond the standard money's worth calculation to also consider the higher risk in private investments, particularly in stocks. Both observations hold whether or not there are individual accounts.

Should Social Security include individual defined-contribution accounts, or should it stay with traditional defined benefits? Panel members are divided on this question, with their differences coming from differences in values, for example, the degree of importance attached to individual versus collective responsibility, and from differences in political predictions, not from differences in economic analyses. Some Panel members are more concerned with the political risks eased by individual accounts, while others are more concerned by the political risks created by individual accounts. In particular, some members think that individual accounts might help the public to agree to allocate more resources to Social Security and to invest in stocks. Individual accounts would have higher administrative costs and expose workers to more economic risks—both in fluctuations in the value of their accounts and in the terms on which benefits would be paid after retirement. Individual accounts would permit different workers to hold different portfolios. The Panel considers a number of implementation and regulation issues for both investment accumulation and benefit payout if there are individual accounts.

The Panel outlines a low-cost, low-services plan for individual accounts, organized by the government. To keep costs low, such a plan would have few investment choices, limited flexibility in the how often workers could adjust their investments, and little investment education for workers. The Panel estimated that it might cost about $25–$50 per participant per year to administer, in addition to current administrative costs. Such a cost would result in a 5–11 percent reduction in accumulated balances for accounts financed by 2 percent of wages or a 2–4 percent reduction for accounts financed by 5 percent of wages.

Having individual accounts that are privately organized, rather than government organized, would provide more services with the accounts and would change the political pressures associated with the accounts. The Panel agrees with the estimate made by the 1994–1996 Social Security Advisory Council that the fees with privately organized individual accounts might average about 1 percent of the accumulated balance each year for accounts financed by 5 percent of wages. Such a fee would reduce the accumulated balance by about 20 percent over a 40-year working career.

Contents

Preface

The National Academy of Social Insurance is pleased to issue this final report of its study panel on Evaluating Issues in Privatizing Social Security. The panel's charge was to address the major technical issues raised by two generic types of Social Security reform proposals involving elements of privatization as part of restoring long term fiscal balance to the program. One type of reform would retain the current defined-benefit structure of Social Security, but build and maintain a larger trust fund partially invested in private securities. The other would represent a marked departure from the current structure of Social Security by establishing individual defined-contribution accounts with investment choices that include private securities. (The panel was not asked to consider more traditional approaches to restoring fiscal balance to the program, since the analytic issues involved therein are already reasonably well understood.) Reform of Social Security has risen to the top of the national agenda since the Academy initiated this project in mid–1996, with concerns about privatization playing a major role in the debate. Thus, the findings of this panel are particularly time-ly and salient.

The project got under way when Michael Boskin of Stanford University and Peter Diamond of MIT agreed to co-chair the panel. The two co-chairs then jointly selected the other panel members for their expertise in actuarial science, economics, law, political science and public policy, as well as their diversity of views on how best to reform Social Security. The co-chairs and panel members disagreed on policy prescriptions; however, their assignment was not to reconcile their differences on major matters of policy, but to clarify and, to the extent feasible, resolve technical concerns about which there is considerable public and even expert confusion in the reform debate. To this end, panel members met nine times over 29 months and devoted many additional hours to drafting and reviewing the language of the final report. They also drew upon papers prepared by various authors for the Academy's 10th annual research conference in January 1998 (published in a volume separately available from the Academy, Framing the Social Security Debate: Values, Politics and Economics) and background materials provided by staff and consultants to the Academy.

I am pleased to report that the areas of general agreement within the panel are extensive and noteworthy. For example, the panel agrees that substantially more advance funding and investment in a diversified portfolio of assets, including stocks and corporate bonds, would increase the national savings rate, strengthen the economy and improve both the fiscal outlook for the program and the rate of return received by future workers on their contributions (taxes) over the long term. The panel also finds that these potential benefits can be accomplished through building larger trust fund reserves under the present structure of Social Security or by moving to defined-contribution individual accounts. It recommends investment of a larger Social Security trust fund in a diversified portfolio, only if a management structure is established to shield portfolio decisions and corporate governance from political pressures. The report further notes that comparable increases in taxes and/or reductions in Social Security benefits are required under either approach to address the current long term deficits faced by the program. Even with respect to the few issues where the panel members remained deeply divided they have performed a useful service. For example, they agreed that their division on the question of whether a reformed Social Security system should include individual investment accounts arises from different valuations of social objectives and views of political realities, rather than disputes over technical matters; and their report provides valuable analyses of numerous issues arising under the major policy alternatives.

As part of its deliberations, the panel agreed that only those conclusions agreed upon by at least three-fourths of the members would receive the panel's imprimatur. Thus, all the findings and recommendations in the report meet this criterion. Also, although three members of the panel (including Mr. Boskin) withdrew from the panel in mid-October 1998, for reasons stated in their memorandum in Appendix B, the report continues to reflect their input into panel deliberations.

I commend this report to all who are interested in a better informed national debate on the future of Social Security. On behalf of the National Academy of Social Insurance, I want to thank all of the panel members for their time, effort, and thoughtfulness in producing it. The panel, in turn, greatly appreciates the efforts of the staff and consultants to the project.

John L. Palmer
President, National Academy of Social Insurance
and Dean, The Maxwell School of Citizenship and Public
Affairs, Syracuse University

Executive Summary

This study explores issues that arise under proposals (1) to build and maintain a sizable Social Security Trust-Fund, partially invested in stocks and corporate bonds, and (2) to introduce individual defined-contribution accounts. The report analyzes the potential effects of such proposals and examines many of the related implementation issues.

The report is organized around five policy questions:

(1) *Should we move toward more advance funding of Social Security obligations, or should these obligations continue to be financed on a pay-as-you-go basis with only a contingency reserve?*

(2) *Should the Social Security Trust Fund invest in a diversified portfolio that includes stocks and corporate bonds, or should it continue to invest only in Treasury bonds? Should Social Security individual accounts have access to diversified portfolios that include stocks and corporate bonds?*

(3) *Should the reformed system create individual (funded defined-contribution) accounts, or should it remain a single collective fund with a defined-benefit formula?*

(4) *If individual accounts are adopted, how much choice should workers be allowed in selecting investments, and in* *the timing and form of payments from the accounts? Should individual accounts be voluntary or mandatory?*

(5) If individual accounts are adopted, should the reformed system move toward private and decentralized collection of contributions, management of investments, and payment of annuities, or should these functions be administered by a government agency (the Treasury or the Social Security Administration)?

Following are the Panel's analyses, findings, and summary views on these five questions. **A recommendation by the Panel is not necessarily unanimous, but has the support of at least three-fourths of the members of the Panel; some qualifications and opposing viewpoints are presented in the text or in notes.** Some technical terms are defined in the Glossary.

The term *privatization* is used in a variety of ways in current Social Security discussions. We distinguish between three terms: advance funding, portfolio diversification, and individual accounts. (1) By *increased advance funding* we mean building and maintaining greater total balances for Social Security, whether this is done in individual accounts or in the Social Security Trust Fund. (2) By *portfolio diversification* we mean investing funds (either from individual accounts or from the Trust Fund) into a broad range of assets, including stocks and corporate bonds. (3) By *individual accounts,* we mean replacing all or part of the current defined-benefit system with a defined-contribution system of individual accounts held in individual workers' names. In the public debate these terms are often linked, but they are conceptually different.

Question 1. Should we move toward more advance funding of Social Security obligations, or should these obligations continue to be financed on a pay-as-you-go basis with only a contingency reserve?

Social Security benefits are financed from tax revenues and from accumulated previous surpluses (including interest returns) in the Social Security Trust Fund. For the near term, taxes exceed benefits, which adds to the value of the Trust Fund and is an important part of the current and projected surpluses in the unified budget. However, the Social Security surplus is projected to end with the retirement of the baby boom generation, and the accumulation of all prior surpluses is projected to be exhausted by the end of 2032. By the latter date, revenue into the funds is projected to cover just three-quarters of the benefits due. Thus, projected revenues for the 75-year period used by Social Security actuaries are not sufficient to pay projected benefits. The projected deficit over the 75-year horizon is 2.19 percent of taxable payroll; further deficits are envisioned beyond the 75-year projection horizon, perhaps doubling the deficit over the indefinite future.

Many combinations of changes to Social Security, if enacted, would result in a projection showing that the Trust Fund would not run out of money during the 75-year projection period. Some of these changes retain the standard goal of maintaining an adequate long-run contingency reserve, that is a Trust Fund at least as large as a single year's expenditures. Some alternatives call for building and maintaining a Trust Fund that accumulates more resources than needed for a one-year contingency reserve level. Other alternatives would accumulate more resources by introducing funded individual defined contribution accounts as part of Social

Security. We will use the term *increased advance funding* to cover the long-run accumulation and maintenance of greater total balances for Social Security, whether this is done within the Trust Fund, within individual accounts, or both.

Increased advance funding would permit lower taxes and/or higher benefits in the future since more assets would produce greater asset returns. A major increase in advance funding, however, would require increased taxes or decreased benefits, or an additional source of revenue in the near term. Therefore, significantly improving the financial value of Social Security for future generations would come at the cost of worsening the financial value of Social Security for current generations or would require that general revenues be devoted to Social Security.

In addition to affecting the workings of Social Security, legislation to increase advance funding will affect the economy. Restoring actuarial balance is likely to increase national savings. Beyond this impact, reforms that involve increased advance funding may increase national savings further, which, in turn, will increase economic growth. However, the impact of increased advance funding on national savings depends not only on the net impact of Social Security changes on the program's funding levels but also on the responses of other savings to these changes. If increased funding of Social Security is to add to national savings, it must not be fully offset from a combination of less savings in the rest of the government budget, less funding for private pensions, and lower individual savings. Advance funding can enhance the financial position of future workers and can increase national savings whether it is done through individual accounts or through a buildup of the Trust Fund. While increased national savings comes at a cost of decreased consumption, the Panel values increased savings, given the current low level of national savings.

If the federal budget does not largely offset the impact on national savings, the Panel recommends increased advance funding of Social Security.

As is discussed under Question 3, some Panel members would like to see increased advance funding through the creation and funding of individual accounts, while some others would like to see it done by building up a large Trust Fund. Another view prefers continuation of pay-as-you-go.

Question 2. Should the Social Security Trust Fund invest in a diversified portfolio that includes stocks and corporate bonds, or should it continue to invest only in Treasury bonds? Should Social Security individual accounts have access to diversified portfolios that include stocks and corporate bonds?

If Social Security is holding assets, whether in a Trust Fund or in individual accounts, then there is a choice as to what assets to hold. After considering individual portfolio choice, we consider Trust Fund portfolio choice, assuming that there is increased advance funding and there are not individual accounts.

Analysts have noted that including stocks in individual accounts or in the Trust Fund would increase the expected rate of return on the portfolios held. In turn, an increased expected return on a portfolio would increase the expected financial return from Social Security taxes, often referred to as money's worth. While other investments can offer a higher expected rate of return than Treasury bonds, it is important to recognize that generally the capital market offers higher expected returns only by having investors take on additional risk. For considering the economic well-being of workers, it is incorrect financial analysis to consider an expected rate of return without considering the risk of the portfolio. While standard money's worth calculations are useful for showing expected financial returns, they are not adequate for considering the economic well-being of workers when comparing policies, such as investment in stocks, that imply different risk characteristics for Social Security benefits. Risk may be considered in a number of ways. Among these are reporting on statistical distributions of prospective outcomes and on money's worth calculations using several rates of return. Consideration of risk shows that the gain in economic well-being from portfolio diversification is generally less than the gain in expected financial return under standard money's worth calculations, which capture only the change in expected return, but not the change in risk.

Many people have diversified portfolios in their non Social-Security retirement accounts. For these people, the composition of Social Security investments is not very important since they can keep their total portfolio more or less the same by adjusting the portfolio outside Social Security to offset changes in risk and expected return coming from changes in portfolios within Social Security. On the other hand, roughly half the working population has little in financial wealth outside Social Security. For these people, inclusion of some stocks in the portfolio with individual accounts or in the Trust Fund is important and the added well-being from the increased expected return is likely to exceed the lessened well-being from the increased risk.

If individual accounts are adopted, the Panel thinks that individuals should be allowed to invest in stocks and corporate bonds.

Currently, the Trust Fund is invested solely in Treasury bonds. Just as is the case for individual and corporate pension investments, in terms solely of risk and return to Social Security covered workers (that is, excluding consideration of social investing and corporate governance issues), a Social Security Trust Fund portfolio consisting entirely of Treasury bonds does not represent an optimal portfolio. The political context of Trust Fund investment in stocks and corporate bonds is considered below.

Without additional net revenue, investment in stocks and corporate bonds by the Trust Fund implies larger sales of Treasury bonds to the private economy than would be the case if the Trust Fund held only Treasury bonds. For example, if the Trust Fund purchases $1 billion in stocks in a year, then the Trust Fund holdings of Treasury bonds will be $1 billion less than if the stocks had not been purchased. If the non-Social Security budget does not change, then the Treasury must borrow this $1 billion from someone else. Similarly, without additional net revenue, diverting some payroll tax revenues into individual accounts would leave less revenue flowing into the Trust Fund; thus, the value of stocks and bonds acquired by individual accounts would be matched initially by a decrease in the value of Treasury bonds held by the Trust Fund. In both cases, the public would end up holding more Treasury bonds and fewer stocks and corporate bonds outside of Social Security. That is, changing the holdings from bonds to stocks is not itself an increase in national savings, but would be an "asset swap" although one that would have effects on the economy.

The gain to workers covered by Social Security from a more diversified portfolio (with or without individual accounts) is of importance beyond any gains to the economy as a whole. With individual account investments, the gain matters particularly for workers who have little in financial wealth. With Trust Fund investments, the gain affects everyone since the use of a defined benefit formula can spread the risk more widely than can be done through the market. The extent of benefit from being able to spread the risk widely depends on how well Congress does it. In evaluating these considerations, it is important to remember that Social Security taxes and benefits are distributed more evenly across the population than personal wealth.

While the actuarial and economic implications of private investment by the Trust Fund are positive if sound investment policies are used, there is serious concern about possible political pressures that would interfere with good investment policies. In addition, there is concern that the government might use its ownership position to unduly influence corporate decisions. Similar issues arise with government-organized individual accounts. Careful design of the governance institution for diversified investment is extremely important in order to help shield fund accumulation, portfolio decisions and corporate governance from political pressures. When the government set up the Thrift Savings Plan, with individual accounts for federal employees, it designed safeguards against political interference, which have been successful to date. These safeguards include limiting investments to index funds.

The Panel recognizes that either Trust Fund investment in stocks or government-organized individual accounts would be a new institution, making it difficult to predict exactly how the institution would work. It is appropriate to build

design features in a new institution that would limit undesirable effects should they develop. Therefore, the Panel
thinks that initial legislation should contain a cap on the fraction of ownership of any firm (through index fund ownership). A cap in the range of 5 to 10 percent seems suitable.
Over time, the cap could be raised if these fears are not realized.

**If the Trust Fund invests in stocks and corporate bonds the
Panel recommends use of a governance structure similar to
that of the Thrift Savings Plan (TSP). If there are individual accounts organized by the government, the Panel also
recommends a governance structure similar to that of the
TSP for investment management of such accounts, since a
number of political issues are similar with both types of
investment.[1] Initial legislation should contain a cap of 5 to
10 percent on the fraction of any firm owned through the
index fund.**

Even with a governance design similar to that of the Thrift
Savings Plan there could be some political interference in
investment decisions or inappropriate influence on corporate governance. Nevertheless, the Panel thinks the Trust
Fund would hold a better portfolio, even after adjusting for
risk, with some investment in stocks and corporate bonds
than with a portfolio invested solely in Treasury bonds. A
dissenting view is that because of the political issues, it
would be better to keep the Trust Fund solely invested in
Treasury bonds.

**If the Trust Fund is sustained as more than a contingency
reserve, and if an investment management structure similar to that of the Thrift Savings Plan is employed, then the**

Panel recommends Trust Fund investment in stocks and corporate bonds provided that the Fund does not own more than 5 to 10 percent the stock of any firm.

There are advantages to portfolio diversification if individual accounts are adopted or if the Trust Fund is diversified. There is disagreement on the Panel about which of these approaches is preferable.

Question 3. Should the reformed system create individual (funded defined-contribution) accounts, or should it remain a single collective fund with a defined-benefit formula?

Individual accounts might be organized in many different ways. We use the term government-organized accounts to denote individual account systems in which the government arranges for both the record keeping for the accounts and the investment management for the funds in the accounts—whether these functions are performed by government agencies or by private firms under contract to the government. An example of government-organized accounts is the federal Thrift Savings Plan (TSP), a pension plan which contracts with a government agency to perform record keeping and with a private firm to do fund management. We use the term privately organized accounts to denote individual account systems in which individuals directly select private firms to do the record keeping and investment management. An example is individual retirement accounts (IRA's), where individuals select their own private financial institution.

Before treating administrative and other aspects of individual accounts, it is worth describing some of the main reasons that individual accounts are recommended as a supplement to or as a partial or full replacement for the current Social Security system as well as some of the main rebuttals.

People who recommend new, mandatory defined contribution accounts see several advantages. First, they think that
many workers are more likely to accept an increase in their
contributions to the retirement system if the workers themselves have clear ownership of the new contributions and
exercise some control over investment choice. The introduction of individual accounts might thus be politically helpful
in providing more advance funding for the retirement system through a payroll tax increase and so increasing national saving.

A second reason for recommending new individual
accounts is that such accounts offer individual workers a
range of choice over how the savings accumulated for their
retirement will be invested, giving workers the freedom to
decide for themselves how much risk to accept in order to
obtain better expected returns on their retirement saving.
Because workers' preferences differ with respect to their tolerance for risk, the welfare of some workers could be
improved if each is permitted to select the combination of
risk and expected return that is most consistent with his or
her preferences.

Third, proponents argue that by leaving decisions about
the allocation of new investment funds and the use of ownership rights up to workers, a system of individual accounts
would reduce the influence of Congress and government
officials over the investment of the funds and the workings
of corporations. Substantial political influence over the
investments would remain, since Congress would wish to
restrict investments to those deemed prudent and appropriate for a retirement fund, and the government would select
the available investments if individual accounts are government organized. But even with this restriction, the division
of funds between Treasury bonds and stocks would be left

up to millions of workers. People who worry about the capacity of government officials to manage private asset accumulation or the tendency to use additional powers would greatly prefer to leave these important investment decisions up to workers rather than place them in the hands of elected or unelected officials.

Finally, many advocates of individual accounts doubt that Congress and the President would refrain from spending a larger accumulation in the Social Security Trust Fund. If a larger reserve were available, or if larger annual surpluses were generated by a policy aimed at building up the Funds, voters and their elected representatives might be tempted to use the extra funds to increase benefits, reduce taxes or boost non-Social-Security spending. The larger build-up in the Trust Fund would not generate a desired result—higher national saving. By accumulating the new reserves in millions of individual accounts rather than a single collective fund, the political temptation to spend the extra accumulation would be lessened. The new assets would be owned by individual contributors and thus harder to spend on benefits for others or non-Social-Security government operations.

People who oppose individual accounts see several disadvantages. First, while some proposals for individual accounts include additional payroll tax revenue, many do not. Opponents are concerned that the political outcome might be that individual accounts are a replacement for part of Social Security, not a supplement.

A second reason for opposing individual accounts is that Social Security, which provides a basic safety net, should provide consistent benefits to all participants to the extent possible. Opponents argue that many workers do not have enough knowledge of investments to make sound choices and some may not wish to do so. In particular, they are concerned about the risks to workers from poor investment choices and from the accident of retiring when the market value of assets is low or the cost of annuities is high. Because of lower administrative cost, they also think that a higher overall rate of return could be achieved without individual accounts.

Third, opponents argue that the risk of social investing exists with individual accounts. They believe there will be pressure on individual workers to make "socially responsible" decisions in both investment choices and exercise of ownership rights, which may not be consistent with choosing the best combination of risk and return. Protection designed into the governance structure for Trust Fund investment would not be available to protect individuals from such pressures.

Finally, those who oppose individual accounts think that there is a risk that the increase in advance funding promised by such accounts cannot be maintained and that an individual account system would lead to undesirable changes in the distribution of benefits. They are concerned that there is likely to be access to individual accounts prior to retirement, or, at least, the availability of a lump sum distribution at retirement age, which may lead to inadequate resources for retired workers and, in particular, a surviving spouse and a decrease in national savings. In the move to individual accounts, benefits may be cut for the disabled, for children after the death of a parent, and for divorcees. Individual accounts may also threaten the extent to which Social Security redistributes benefits to low income workers.

Having described the most common arguments for and against introducing individual accounts, we turn now to administrative issues raised by such accounts and a more

detailed consideration of the economic and political arguments advanced for and against such accounts.

Administrative Structure and Costs[2]

The implementation and maintenance of individual
accounts involve many steps. The Report contains a task list
detailing many of these steps. When comparing different
cost estimates for individual accounts, it is important to
understand which steps are included in the cost estimate and
which are assumed to be performed and paid for separately,
whether by government, individuals or employers. The
Panel urges that all proposals to establish individual
accounts spell out which aspects of collection, accumulation,
asset management, and distribution would be done by the
government, employers, asset management firms, and individuals. This will help assure that different cost estimates are
comparable in that they are costing the same set of tasks.

Almost all proposals with individual accounts envision
continuing some defined benefit retirement system as well
as continuing disability and young survivor benefits using
the current administrative structure. Therefore, the lowest-
cost method of designing individual accounts would build
as much as possible on the existing Social Security structure.
The report outlines an example of such a system.

We cannot be sure what it would cost to add a low-
cost/low-services system of government-organized individual accounts or what services would be legislated (which
would affect the cost). If the costs were the same as for the
Thrift Savings Plan, the government's administrative costs of
the reformed system (including individual accounts and the
remaining defined benefit program) would more than double current Social Security administrative costs, which are

$16 per person (workers and beneficiaries) or $3.4 billion in 1997. Costs of a low cost/low services system may well be considerably higher than TSP costs. As a rough order of magnitude, costs for the individual account portion of the reformed system could be $25–50 per worker per year in addition to the cost of the existing system. Switching to private organization of accounts as a method of providing wider choice of investments and making available more services would also raise overall costs beyond those of government-organized accounts, as is discussed under Question 5.

To put this range of costs into perspective, let us compare the annual costs with annual deposits. In 1997, mean taxable Social Security earnings were approximately $23,000. If 1.6 percent of workers' earnings went to individual accounts, a $25–50 range of costs charged to the account would be equal to 7–14 percent of new contributions for the mean earner (equivalent to a "front load" charge); with 2 percent accounts, the front load would be 5–11 percent; with 5 percent accounts, it would be 2–4 percent; and with 10 percent accounts, it would be 1–2 percent. These calculations would be the same for workers at all earnings levels if charges were the same percentage for all workers. If charges reflected some of the fixed costs of accounts, the load would be larger for low earners and smaller for high earners.

Another way to describe these charges is to ask what charge as a fraction of assets under management would cover these costs on a lifetime basis, assuming that the cost grew with average wages. With 2 percent accounts, an annual $25–50 charge would be equivalent to a 25–50 basis point charge on assets under management over a 40-year career; with 5 percent accounts, a 10–20 basis point charge. That mean taxable earnings of Social Security covered workers is much lower than that of workers with 401(k) plan savings is relevant for interpreting these figures.

In contrast, direct Trust Fund investment in stocks and corporate bonds would cost very little, roughly 0.5 basis points of the portion of the Trust Fund invested in these securities. Therefore, because of lower administrative costs, the implicit rate of return on Social Security with Trust Fund investment would be higher than the return that could be achieved with individual accounts if the Social Security Trust Fund were invested and maintained in a similar portfolio. Administrative costs are not the sole basis for evaluating individual accounts, as is discussed below.

Economics of Accumulation

The economic effects of an increase in advance funding would be similar whether the system has individual accounts or not, although the politics would be different.

Distribution of Risk

With individual accounts, workers directly bear the risk associated with market fluctuations in the value of their accumulations and in the terms on which annuities are available when annuitization occurs. There is risk in the returns on Trust Fund investment as well. However, there is the opportunity to spread the risk of market fluctuations more broadly and evenly across age cohorts by making changes in taxes and benefits for future taxpayers and beneficiaries.

One of the potential advantages of individual accounts is that different workers could hold different portfolios enabling those less averse to risk to bear more of it. Also, individual accounts might not face the same level of restrictions on the choice of assets and degree of stock market investment as with Trust Fund investment. The gains from individual choice would depend on the extent to which people were successful in selecting portfolios suitable for their degree of risk aversion.

Money's Worth

One of the most popular arguments put forward in favor of individual accounts is that moving to a system of individual accounts would raise the rate of return on Social Security for all. The typical approach compares the historical rate of return on U.S. capital markets to the projected rate of return on Social Security, observes that Social Security returns are much lower, and then concludes that a shift to individual accounts would enable all households to attain the higher rates of return attainable on U.S. capital markets.

However, comparing a market return on a portfolio with a return on taxes is comparing apples and oranges. Comparing a benefit that could be financed by saving all of payroll taxes with projected Social Security benefits is similarly misleading. Proper comparisons of how a shift to individual accounts would affect projected money's worth are more complex than simply calculating the expected return on asset portfolios that might be held in individual accounts.

First, the existing system provides life insurance in the event of early death of a worker, disability insurance, and retirement benefits for previously disabled workers. Preserving these important functions would use part of payroll tax revenue. Second, if the current Social Security system were to be fully replaced, it would be necessary to recognize the large unfunded obligation of Social Security. That is, some portion of current and future Social Security revenues, or some other revenue source, is needed to pay benefits to those already retired and those who will retire during any transition to a different system. This cost cannot be avoided if the expectations of retirees and those nearing retirement are to be met. Neither the unfunded obligation nor the costs of financing it go away by diverting revenue from the defined-benefit part of Social Security to individual accounts. These costs need to be paid even if a switch is made to an individual account system. If all of the cost of the unfunded obligation were allocated to individual accounts, it would completely eliminate the rate of return advantage of individual accounts. Money's worth calculations need to reflect an entire proposal, including transition costs.

More advance funding going into individual accounts or the Social Security Trust Fund would eventually improve standard money's worth calculations for future workers, but would worsen it for cohorts that would finance the increase in advance funding.

Benefit Structure

Currently, Social Security provides disability benefits as well as retirement benefits for previously disabled workers and their surviving spouses. It also provides benefits for minor children in the event of the death of a parent. Introduction of individual accounts needs to be carefully integrated with both disability benefits and benefits for children after the death of a parent. While careful review of the level of disability and young survivor benefits should be part of any reform of Social Security, change in the level of these benefits should not happen as an accidental byproduct of reform of the retirement benefit system.

Currently, Social Security provides benefits to aged divorced spouses of retired workers and aged surviving divorced spouses based on lifetime earnings of the former spouse. Divorced women are among the poorest of the elderly. Introduction of individual accounts must consider carefully the rules governing disposition of the accounts in the event of a divorce and the effect on elderly unmarried divorcees.

Currently, Social Security provides benefits to aged surviving spouses. On average, elderly widows and widowers are considerably less well-off than elderly couples. Introduction of individual accounts must consider carefully the effect on elderly surviving spouses.

The Panel thinks protection of a lower-earning spouse is important and needs to be addressed in any reform proposal. If a system does not mandate considerable benefits for a divorced or surviving spouse, at least it should have a division of accounts between spouses in some form.

Legislation requiring that the funds accumulated in individual accounts be annuitized at or after retirement (and that these annuities be joint and survivor annuities) might be difficult to sustain politically as the public image of Social Security changed from that of a provider of monthly benefits to that of (partially) an organizer or individually owned accounts. This could leave retired workers and in particular widowed spouses exposed to substantial longevity risk.

The Panel thinks that having higher replacement rates for low income workers is an important aspect of Social Security. For any combined system, preservation of the redistributive characteristics of the program could be

accomplished through a combination of the progressivity of the remaining defined benefit portion and additional contributions to individual accounts of low earners.

Individual Values

The Panel recognizes that the choice between individual accounts and a fully defined-benefit system depends on more than actuarial and economic outcomes. Individual values play a role as well, since this choice involves a tension between a principle of individual responsibility, ownership and choice and a competing principle of collective responsibility that involves the sharing of costs and risks.

Political Concerns

In addition to the economic implications of using a (partially) defined-contribution as opposed to (fully) defined-benefit approach to Social Security, there is a relationship between these approaches to reform and possible political outcomes. Legislation actually adopted is likely to be a compromise that differs from any single proposal put forth. Thus analysis needs to consider what Congress is likely to legislate and how it will change the program over time. Concern about future legislation is usefully considered in three different ways. First, economic and demographic changes are likely to differ from whatever is projected when legislation is passed. Responses to those deviations from projections are likely to be different with than without individual accounts. Second, individual accounts may alter the frequency and degree to which future taxes and benefits are changed in response to changes in the balance of political pressures. Third, the Social Security institutions themselves are likely to generate political pressures that may lead to changes in Social Security. Indeed, some political approaches may not be viable in the sense that their legislation generates political pressures which, in time, will defeat the primary purpose behind the initial legislation.

Taking into account all of the issues involved in setting up individual accounts, the Panel is divided as to whether individual accounts should be part of Social Security reform.

The Panel's split on whether to recommend individual accounts does not arise primarily from differences in economic analyses. Rather, it derives from the different weights placed on different values by the Panel members, as well as from different political predictions. We now gather together the key arguments that have led different Panel members to different conclusions. Supporters and opponents of individual accounts do not necessarily give weight to all of the reasons presented here.

Reasons for recommending individual accounts:

1. Individual accounts may be more likely to be financed with additional resources (and so add to national savings).

2. If advance funding were held in a central Trust Fund, it might not be sustained, but might be used for some other purpose, such as an increase in benefits or other spending, as in the past.

3. Stocks held in a central Trust Fund might be used to directly influence corporate decision-making based on concerns other than financial risk and return; and investment policy might be based on concerns other than financial risk and return.

4. Legislation without individual accounts might not restore the confidence of many, particularly younger, workers in the future of Social Security, affecting support for the program.

5. Individual accounts encourage individual responsibility and allow individual ownership and individual choice.

6. Individual accounts permit people with different degrees of risk aversion to hold different portfolios.

7. Individual accounts may discourage tax evasion and increase incentives to participate in the system.

8. Individual accounts may reduce the frequency of certain kinds of Social Security legislation and better insulate some individuals from the risk of future legislated benefit cuts.

Reasons for and against specifically government-organized individual accounts:

1. Government-organized accounts would cost less to administer than privately organized accounts and would give workers fewer investment options.

2. Stocks held in government-organized individual accounts might be used to directly influence corporate decision-making based on concerns other than financial risk and return; and investment policy might be based on concerns other than financial risk and return.

3. By providing less in services than is common with many 401(k) plans, government-organized accounts might lead some people to view the government as inefficient in its provision of retirement income, because they were not fully aware of the lower per capita costs.

Reasons for opposing individual accounts:

1. Individual accounts would increase administrative costs, increase the exposure of workers to market risks, and expose workers to the risk of poor investment choices.

2. Early access to individual accounts and the receipt of benefits as a lump-sum might not preserve adequate benefits for workers and for surviving spouses. This would also decrease the contribution to national savings.

3. The creation and possible later growth of individual accounts might be financed, in part, by lowering benefits in the disability and/or young survivors insurance programs.

4. The creation and possible later growth of individual accounts might result in an erosion of the benefit levels provided to those with low earnings.

5. Individual accounts would undercut the sense of community responsibility and shared concerns embodied in Social Security; large variation in benefits between members of different cohorts employing the same investment strategy is undesirable.

6. Individual accounts might be financed by a diversion of resources that would otherwise go to the Trust Fund, so that they would not contribute to increased national savings.

7. Restoring actuarial balance in the existing system might restore workers' confidence in the future of Social Security; by diverting revenues and introducing new risks, individual accounts might not improve confidence either in the remaining defined benefit portion of Social Security or in the overall system.

8. By possibly diverting resources from the Trust Fund to individual accounts, the defined benefit will be less well financed and more likely to have financial difficulty requiring legislation.

Panel members weighing these values, political predictions, and economic implications differently have reached different conclusions as to the desirability of individual accounts. Some of these considerations weigh more or less heavily depending on details of a proposal, especially the source of funding.

Question 4. If individual accounts are adopted, how much choice should workers be allowed in selecting investments, and in the timing and form of payments from the accounts? Should individual accounts be voluntary or mandatory?

Investment Choice

The Panel is concerned that many investors may fail to understand the risk characteristics of investments.

The Panel thinks that if there are individual accounts organized by the government, individuals should have choices that include government bonds (including inflation-protected bonds) and separate index funds containing private bonds, stocks in the United States, and possibly investments abroad.[3]

The Panel thinks that if there are individual accounts organized by private firms, the choices should be restricted to widely diversified mutual funds and guaranteed products, such as federal government bonds (including inflation-protected bonds), stable value funds and certificates of deposit (CDs).[4]

Restrictions on privately organized investment choices made available under Social Security will lead to new regulatory oversight of financial institutions. In addition, there will be calls for the government to insure promised returns for mandated savings that are invested in guaranteed products, particularly after a financial disappointment. Guarantees arranged in advance, including a premium charged for the guarantee, are preferable to bailouts after the fact.

Benefit Choice

Two issues arise when considering individual choice about the provision of retirement income: (1) the choices individuals make for themselves and (2) the protection of spouses in the event of the death of a worker. Before moving toward individual choice, its effect on the economic position of surviving spouses needs to be assessed very carefully.

Left to their own devices, relatively few people take advantage of private annuities, exposing themselves to the risk of outliving their assets. The current provision of monthly Social Security benefits reduces the importance of this risk. We do not have sufficient historical evidence to know whether people would voluntarily annuitize their individual accounts sufficiently to roughly maintain the annuitization level currently provided by Social Security monthly benefits.

The Panel thinks retirees should not be able to take all of their retirement benefits as a lump sum. Annuitization (through either a defined-benefit system or mandated annuitization of at least part of accumulations) or restrictions on the rate of monthly withdrawal should be part of the system.

In addition to the issue of annuitization, evidence from the United Kingdom suggests that people purchasing annuities do not purchase inflation protection when they have the opportunity. While a predictable rate of inflation can be handled by a given annual rate of increase in nominal benefits, the unpredictability of inflation makes indexing to inflation of greater value.

The Panel thinks that mandated annuities should be real annuities, that is, annuities indexed for inflation.

Given the choice, many workers tend to select single-life as opposed to joint-and-survivor annuities that continue payment to a worker's spouse after the worker's death. The degree to which workers choose joint-and-survivor annuitization is very sensitive to the way choices are presented to them.

The protection of a lower-earning spouse is important, and if a system does not mandate considerable benefits for a surviving spouse, at least it should have a division of accounts between spouses in some form.

Voluntary Individual Accounts

In terms of implementation, regulation and enforcement, voluntary accounts have all the cost and design issues of mandatory accounts, plus some additional costs as a consequence of the need to receive, process, monitor and correct reports of whether an individual has chosen to use an individual account. Moreover, some economies of scale are lost as a result of less than full selection of accounts. Allowing voluntary diversion of payroll taxes from the defined benefit program to individual accounts would have a serious adverse-selection risk. Unless the rules governing the decrease in defined benefits for those who opt out correctly adjust for this risk, voluntary accounts might worsen the financial position of the defined benefit portion of Social

Security. Similarly, voluntary opt-out and risky investment choices by those possibly eligible for Supplemental Security Income (SSI) benefits might increase the cost of the SSI program. In any case, benefit rules to account for selection risk would be either very complex or very approximate.

The Panel does not recommend allowing voluntary diversion of payroll tax contributions from the defined-benefit program to individual accounts.[5]

Question 5. If individual accounts are adopted, should the reformed system move toward private and decentralized collection of contributions, management of investments, and payment of annuities, or should these functions be administered by a government agency (the Treasury or the Social Security Administration)?

Collection

If there were government-organized accounts, there would be no point in having private collection of deposits. If there were privately organized accounts, the deposits could be collected by the federal government and handed over to financial institutions (possibly less a fee for the costs of collection and transmittal). Alternatively, the funds could go directly from employers or employees to private financial institutions. Direct deposits by employers or employees would also require substantial regulatory and enforcement costs for the government to assure that the accounts are established and maintained and funds are deposited in a timely manner.

The Panel thinks the direct economic gains from mandatory direct deposits by employers would not be worth the increase in cost, at least until and if widespread adoption of technology led to a substantial decrease in costs.

Organization of Accounts

Accounts could be government- or privately organized. Since much of administrative costs are fixed costs, the Panel thinks the charges for privately organized individual accounts would be larger, in percentage terms, for smaller than for larger accounts unless uniform percentage charges were required.

Currently, banks, insurance companies, and mutual funds often require minimum account balances and offer lower per dollar charges for larger accounts than smaller ones. Thus, the primary impact of regulation requiring uniform percentage charges would be the requirement that financial institutions accept all accounts on the same terms.

If there are individual accounts organized by private financial institutions, the Panel recommends regulations that would require any financial institution accepting such accounts (1) to apply the same charges (per dollar of deposits and per dollar of account balances) for all workers, and (2) to accept all workers who wished to use the institution, regardless of the size of their accounts.[6]

The Panel thinks that the estimate of the Advisory Council on Social Security—of an annual charge of 1 percent of the account balance, for Personal Security Accounts funded by 5 percent of the payroll tax—is roughly correct on average. This figure is similar to fees paid on average with private investments today. With smaller accounts (2 or 3 percent of payroll), charges would be higher in percentage terms since much of the cost would be a fixed cost per account.

A 1 percent per year fee for funds under management corresponds to roughly a 20 percent decrease in the accumulation in an account at the end of a 40-year career, as compared with an account without charges. In contrast, with government-organized accounts funded by 5 percent of payroll, an annual charge of $25–50 (that grew at the same rate as wages) would be equivalent to a front load of roughly 2–4 percent for the average worker and would lower the value of accounts by 2–4 percent, considerably less than the roughly 20 percent reduction from a 1 percent of assets annual fee. However, as discussed above, the administrative costs are not the sole basis for evaluating individual accounts or for evaluating the method of organization. The level of services provided with privately organized accounts would be greater than with low cost/low services government-organized accounts. Moreover, government-organized accounts would not have the costs of competition—advertising and brokers' commissions.

Annuitization

Annuitization of individual accounts might be accomplished in three different ways—(1) the federal government could decide what benefits to pay for given levels of accumulation; (2) the federal government could contract with private providers to receive accumulated funds in return for paying the annuities; or (3) individuals could be left free to contract with insurance companies on their own, purchasing annuities from their accounts. With the second approach, annuities would be priced on a group basis; with the third, on an individual basis. In insurance markets generally, group products are considerably less expensive than individual products. Administrative costs of privately supplied individual annuities (ignoring issues of adverse selection) are estimated to be 5 to 10 percent of the purchase price currently, varying with the nature of the portfolio used for comparison purposes. The Panel thinks this is a ballpark figure for what individual mandated annuities would cost. Currently, adverse selection results in mortality experience for annuity purchasers that adds roughly 10 percent to the price of annuities as compared with population mortality experience. Potentially an increased demand for annuities could lead to economies of scale and less adverse selection. However, it is difficult to know whether the market for annuities would expand significantly (decreasing adverse selection)without a mandate.

In light of the cost issue, the Panel thinks that if annuitization is mandated and if it is provided by private firms, the annuities should be supplied as group annuities to the extent possible. This could be done by market bidding for groups with government-organized individual accounts. With privately organized accounts, the government could encourage or mandate the formation of groups.

The Panel does not take a stand on whether individual accounts would best be organized by the government or by private firms. The Panel recognizes that the initial implementation of a privately organized individual account system would be more expensive and difficult than initial implementation of a government-organized account system.

Recognizing all of the issues involved, including the difficulty of initial implementation, the Panel thinks that if individual accounts are created, they should start as gov-

ernment-organized accounts. **Within a few years of full implementation, there should be serious consideration of a shift to privately organized accounts.**[7]

Timing of Legislation

Prompt legislative action will permit more gradual tax and/or benefit changes and allow more advance notice of benefit changes. The longer the delay in legislation, the more difficult the economic and political problems of reform will become.

The Panel urges that legislation restoring actuarial balance and containing whatever reforms are agreed upon be passed as soon as possible.

Introduction

This study explores issues that arise under proposals (1) to build and maintain a sizable Social Security Trust Fund partially invested in stocks and corporate bonds, and (2) to introduce individual funded defined-contribution accounts. The President has called for a national dialogue on Social Security reform, and proposals including the elements discussed herein are coming from many sources, including newly filed bills in Congress. The report analyzes the potential effects of such proposals and examines many of the related implementation issues. It is thereby intended to contribute to the debate on whether to adopt these reforms, as well as to support the design of any associated legislation. The discussion is largely at a generic level, although some possibilities are explored in detail.

Background

Social Security is the nation's largest government program. It provides retirement income, and disability and survivor benefits, to 44 million people. About one-third of retirees rely almost exclusively on Social Security for retirement income. The program is financed by payroll taxes, which are second only to the individual income tax as source of federal revenue. (Trustees' Report, 1998) Because of its size, Social Security affects economic well-being beyond its direct impact on beneficiaries and tax payers. For example, Social Security is an important contributor to the trend to earlier retirement and to the low level of private savings, which decrease national output.

Because Social Security is so large and important, and in many ways complex, various proposals to change some of its features would be worth considering even if the system were in long-run actuarial balance, i.e., even if projected revenues matched projected outlays. However, the impetus to consider reform proposals is undoubtedly greatly enhanced by the large projected long-run actuarial deficit in Social Security. The combination of the impending retirement of the baby boom generation beginning about 2010, plus the likely continued increase in life expectancy, is projected to decrease the ratio of workers to beneficiaries, from about 3.4 workers per beneficiary today to about 2.0 workers per beneficiary in 2030 (Trustees' Report, 1998). This demographic change is a large part of the story behind the projected long-run deficit.

Without remedial action, the baseline (intermediate)[8] projections indicate that tax revenues will be less than benefit payments beginning in 2013, the Trust Fund[9] balance will begin to decline in 2021, and Trust Fund assets will be depleted in 2032 (Trustees' Report, 1998). By 2032, revenue into the funds is projected to cover just three-quarters of the benefits due. The projected deficit over the 75-year horizon is 2.19 percent of taxable payroll. Further deficits are envisioned beyond the 75-year projection horizon, perhaps doubling the deficit over the indefinite future.

The short-term revenue surpluses in the Trust Fund are an important part of the current and projected surpluses in the unified federal budget. Thus, Social Security reform is part of the debate on how to handle those surpluses. Social Security reform could also contribute to increased national savings, an area of ongoing concern. Moreover, the exceptionally high returns in the stock market over the last few years naturally have contributed to public interest in linking retirement incomes with stock market returns. Creation of individual accounts in other countries (including Britain, Chile, Mexico and Sweden), the forthcoming investment of social security reserves in private securities in Canada, and the growing importance of defined contribution private pensions in the United States affect understanding and public perceptions. Thus the reform debate involves a number of important issues beyond the projected actuarial imbalance and the need to have a good system for providing income to workers and their families at retirement, or at the death, or disability of a worker.

What do we mean by Social Security privatization?[10]

The term *privatization* is used in a variety of ways in current Social Security discussions. Before proceeding, it is useful to draw a clear distinction among three terms that are not always distinguished: advance funding, portfolio diversification, and individual accounts. (1) By *increased advance funding* we mean building and maintaining greater total balances for Social Security, whether this is done in individual accounts or in the Social Security Trust Fund. (2) By *portfolio diversification* we mean investing funds (either from individual accounts or from the Trust Fund) into a broad range of assets. These assets might include stocks and bonds issued by U. S. corporations, and foreign securities, in addition to the Treasury bonds now used exclusively by the Social Security Trust Fund. At the present time, the focus is on diversifying into stocks. (3) By *individual accounts*, we mean replacing all or part of the current defined-benefit system with a defined-contribution system of individual accounts held in individual workers' names.

In the public debate these terms are often linked, but they are conceptually different. Suppose the Social Security system had begun as a forced saving plan in which all workers were obliged to set aside money for their retirement which would be put into their own individual accounts invested in a balanced portfolio of stocks and bonds. Then, from the beginning, the system would have been completely advance funded, with a diversified portfolio and individual accounts. In contrast, today, Social Security has a target of only a contingency reserve that is fully invested in Treasury bonds. While individual earnings records are the basis for determining benefits, assets are not accumulated in individual accounts.

Social Security reform could change any one of these three categories without changing the other two. For example, the Trust Fund could invest in stocks as well as Treasury bonds, thus diversifying the portfolio without setting up individual accounts. Alternatively, workers could be given individual accounts in which the money was always invested in Treasury bonds, thus having individual accounts without diversifying the portfolio. It is also possible to increase advance funding without involving individual accounts; taxes could be raised or benefits cut and the proceeds could be put into the Trust Fund. Conversely, people could be given individual accounts without increasing the overall funding of Social Security. Chile is the best-known example of a country whose program has all three features, but one can have some of the features without the others, as has been done elsewhere.

Separate from these three concepts is the role to be played by individual choice since one could set up an advance funded system with a diversified portfolio and individual accounts, but no individual choice, as was the case in Singapore.

Report Scope and Organization

The report is organized around five policy questions. The focus is on the long-run design of alternative retirement income systems, not the issues involved in designing a transition from the current system to various alternatives. The five policy questions that serve to organize the report are as follows:

(1) *Should we move toward more advance funding of Social Security obligations, or should these obligations continue to be financed on a pay-as-you-go basis with only a contingency reserve?*

(2) *Should the Social Security Trust Fund invest in a diversified portfolio that includes stocks and corporate bonds, or should it continue to invest only in Treasury bonds? Should Social Security individual accounts have access to diversified portfolios that include stocks and corporate bonds?*

(3) *Should the reformed system create individual (funded defined-contribution) accounts, or should it remain a single collective fund with a defined-benefit formula?*

(4) *If individual accounts are adopted, how much choice should workers be allowed in selecting investments, and in the timing and form of payments from the accounts? Should individual accounts be voluntary or mandatory?*

(5) *If individual accounts are adopted, should the reformed system move toward private and decentralized collection of contributions, management of investments, and payment of annuities, or should these functions be administered by a government agency (the Treasury or the Social Security Administration)?*

Following are the Panel's findings, conclusions, and summary views on these five questions. The highlights of the Panel's analytical findings are in italics. The policy recommendations of the Panel are in bold. **A recommendation by the Panel is not necessarily unanimous, but has the support of at least three-fourths of the members of the Panel; some qualifications and opposing viewpoints are presented in the text or in notes.** Some technical terms are defined in the Glossary.

Question 1

Advance Funding vs. Pay-As-You-Go

Should we move toward more advance funding of Social Security obligations, or should these obligations continue to be financed on a pay-as-you-go basis with only a contingency reserve?

1.1 Social Security Finances

Social Security benefits are financed from tax revenues and from accumulated previous surpluses (including interest returns) in the Social Security Trust Fund. Currently, Social Security revenues exceed expenditures. This surplus adds to the value of the Trust Fund. However, this surplus is projected to end with the retirement of the baby boom generation, and accumulation of all prior surpluses are projected to be exhausted by the end of 2032.

There are many combinations of changes to Social Security which, if enacted, would result in a projection showing that the Trust Fund would not run out of money during the 75-year projection period. Some of these changes retain the standard goal of maintaining an adequate long-run contingency reserve, that is, a Trust Fund at least as large as a single year's expenditures. Some alternatives call for building and maintaining a Trust Fund that accumulates more resources than needed for a one-year contingency reserve level. Other alternatives would accumulate more resources by introducing funded individual defined contribution accounts as part of Social Security.[11] We will use the term *increased advance funding* to cover the long-run accumulation and maintenance of greater total balances for Social Security whether this is done within the Trust Fund, within individual accounts, or both.

Increased advance funding will affect Social Security and also may affect national savings and so the growth of the economy, as is discussed below. In this section we consider primarily the advantages and disadvantages of increased advance funding that are common to systems with and without individual accounts. Under Question 3, we focus on what is different with and without individual accounts.

The level of Social Security funding is the result of the history of tax revenues, expenditure levels, and the investment returns on existing funds. That is, the funding at the start of a year equals the funding at the start of the previous year plus the investment returns on those funds plus tax revenues minus expenditures. Thus, to increase the level of funding, compared with some chosen baseline, one needs to have more tax revenues,[12] lower benefits,[13] or higher investment returns on the fund, or to allocate some general revenues to Social Security beyond what is presumed with the chosen baseline. Under Question 2, we will consider the choice of investments to be held by Social Security, with and without individual accounts. We note that simply changing the portfolio of the Trust Fund from one fully invested in Treasury bonds to a diversified portfolio would not be enough, by itself, to restore actuarial balance—additional changes would also be needed. In this section, we focus on increasing advance funding by changing tax revenues and/or benefit payments.

Increasing accumulated surpluses and maintaining them into the future in the Trust Fund or in individual accounts, referred to as increased advance funding, would permit lower taxes and/or higher benefits in the future since there would be more assets and greater asset returns. A major increase in advance funding, however, would require increased taxes or decreased benefits, or an additional source of revenue in the near term.

Therefore, significantly improving the financial value of Social Security for future generations would come at the cost of worsening the financial value of Social Security for current generations or would require that general revenues be devoted to Social Security advance funding can enhance the financial position of future workers and can increase national saving whether it is done through individual accounts or through a buildup of the Trust Fund.

To examine the impact of advance funding on the economic resources of future retirees, it is not sufficient just to consider the determination of Social Security benefits. Since increased advance funding could reduce corporate pensions and private savings, such an offset would decrease the impact of advance funding on retirement income. This issue is discussed below in the context of the parallel issue of national savings. Also discussed below in section 3.6 is the effect of increased advance funding on future legislation affecting both Social Security and the non-Social Security budget.

1.2 Increased Advance Funding and National Savings

Restoring actuarial balance is likely to increase national savings, by some combination of increasing net revenues and decreasing projected future benefits. Beyond this impact, reforms that involve increased advance funding may increase national savings further, which, in turn, would increase economic growth. The impact of increased advance funding on national savings depends not only on the net impact on funding levels but also on the responses of other savings to Social Security changes. These include responses by the federal government in its decisions on the non-Social Security portion of its budget, by corporations in their pension design, and by individual savers in response to both government and corporate changes. If increased funding of Social Security is to add to national savings, there must not be a full offset from a combination of less savings in the rest of the government budget, less funding for private pensions, and lower individual savings. We turn first to the rest of the government budget.

Increased advance funding of Social Security could result in legislation of a larger deficit in the non-Social Security portion of the budget.[14] In part, the link between the Social Security and non-Social Security portions of the budget comes from consideration of the unified budget. While changes in how the unified budget is measured may well be part of Social Security reform legislation, it is useful to briefly consider how current measurement is likely to be extended to new budget allocations. Any allocation of general revenues into individual accounts would likely be considered a budget expenditure and so a decrease in the projected surplus in the unified budget. Similarly, increased payroll tax revenue flowing into individual accounts and future investment returns in these accounts would not be part of the unified budget. In contrast to the measurement with individual accounts, any allocation of general revenues into Treasury bonds held by the Trust Fund would not affect the surplus in the unified budget. Similarly, increased payroll tax revenue flowing into Trust Fund holdings of Treasury bonds would increase the unified budget surplus. However, any allocation of general revenues used to purchase corporate stocks held by the Trust Fund would be an expenditure and so a decrease in the surplus in the unified budget. Similarly, increased payroll tax revenue flowing into Trust Fund holdings of stocks would not change the unified budget surplus. Future investment returns of the Trust Fund would be revenue for the unified budget, which would be offset to the extent they were reinvested in stocks.

It is difficult to predict how Congress would change the rest of the budget in response to Social Security legislation. There has been no simple link between past Social Security surpluses and deficits and legislation determining the deficit in the rest of the government budget. In addition, the Panel recognizes that Congress may well change budget reporting rules as part of a package that reforms Social Security. Indeed the impact on national savings is likely to be among the considerations when Congress shapes the package of both Social Security reform and the non–Social Security budget.

Nevertheless, some analysts worry that a large Trust Fund will result in future legislators using the money to increase benefits, or decrease social security taxes, both of which would reduce the fund, or simply to increase current government expenditures that would not have been undertaken otherwise. If these expenditures are not investments, the larger Trust Fund will not have resulted in a sustained increase in national capital. This issue is discussed further under Question 3, where consideration is given to possible responses of future Congresses to a buildup of greater total balances for Social Security either in individual accounts or in the Trust Fund.

Corporations may alter their pension plans in response to legislation that changes the advance funding of Social Security.[15] Pension design might respond to changes in payroll taxes and/or to changes in legislated benefits. Indeed some corporate pension plans are integrated with Social Security in a form so that some changes in Social Security would automatically trigger changes in the corporate pension; changes which would then be reviewed and possibly revised. Some large employers have traditionally used total retirement income replacement rate models in designing employer-sponsored retirement plans. If Social Security reform did not significantly change the levels of benefits provided through the government mandated tier of the retirement system, firms that continued to rely on traditional replacement rate targets might not change employer-sponsored benefits. It is also possible that some corporations would respond differently to the creation of defined contribution accounts (which resemble 401(k) plans) than to changes in defined benefits (which resemble corporate defined benefit plans). Unfortunately, there has been little study of how corporations respond to changes in Social Security. Thus the Panel does not have a firm basis for projecting whether increased advance funding for Social Security would result in decreased advance funding of private pensions.

Individual savings respond to payroll taxes, to perceptions of future benefits, and possibly, to the form in which Social Security is organized. Unlike corporate responses, there has been considerable study of the impact of Social Security on private savings. Raising payroll taxes would have a sizable impact on private consumption. Since many workers do little individual savings, most of any increase in payroll taxes is likely to come from consumption. Thus an increase in payroll taxes that is used for increased advance funding is not likely to be offset much by changes in private savings. Similarly, increased advance funding that comes from decreases in benefits for current retirees will reduce consumption and not have much of an offset on saving. Future increases in advance funding from decreased future benefits would not directly affect government savings in the short run, but some people would save more in anticipation of lower benefits, resulting in some immediate increase in national savings. However, the size of this response depends on the extent to which legislation lowers benefits below anticipated benefit decreases. A similar analysis holds for legislation of future tax increases. Another question, on which there is not direct evidence, is whether a change from defined benefit to defined contribution would change perceptions of retirement financing and so change savings. On the one hand, since individual accounts closely resemble 401(k)s and IRAs, a shift to individual accounts might lead some workers to decrease their use of these accounts. On the other hand some workers who currently do little savings might change their habits and start saving more after their experience with individual accounts.

Similarly, increased advance funding that comes from transfers from general revenues would have some effect, lowering private savings in anticipation of greater future benefits than without the transfer. The overall effect on national savings also depends on what else the government would have done with the general revenues.

In sum, an important step in relating increased advance funding to increased national savings is the behavior of the rest of the government budget. In particular, increasing the debt held by the public to provide additional funding for Social Security would not contribute to national savings.

Increased advance funding of Social Security can increase national savings and thereby national income, provided that the federal budget does not largely offset the impact. While increased national savings comes at a cost of decreased consumption, the Panel values increased savings, given the current low level of national savings.

If the federal budget does not largely offset the impact on national savings, the Panel recommends increased advance funding of Social Security.[16]

Beneath this consensus lie some disagreements. As is discussed in answer to Question 3, some Panel members would like to see advance funding through the creation and funding of individual accounts, while some others would like to see it done by building up and maintaining a large Trust Fund. Another view prefers continuation of pay-as-you-go financing. The Panel recommendation to increase advance funding leads to the question of the form in which to hold the extra funds. With either individual accounts or a Trust Fund, there are portfolio choices to be made. We consider these next.

Question 2   Investment Policy

Should the Social Security Trust Fund invest in a diversified portfolio that includes stocks and corporate bonds, or should it continue to invest only in Treasury bonds? Should Social Security individual accounts have access to diversified portfolios that include stocks and corporate bonds?

If Social Security is holding assets, whether in a Trust Fund or in individual accounts, then there is a choice as to what assets to hold. We begin by considering individual portfolio choices both inside and outside individual accounts. Then, to discuss Trust Fund portfolio choice, we consider a setting where there is advance funding through the Trust Fund and there are no individual accounts.[17]

2.1 Individual Portfolio Choice and Returns

Corporate stocks and bonds have a higher expected return than Treasury bonds because they are riskier. This higher expected return is called a "risk premium." A portfolio invested 100 percent in Treasury bonds does not take on this risk and thus receives no risk premium.[18]

While other investments can offer a higher expected rate of return than Treasury bonds, it is important to recognize that generally the capital market offers higher expected returns only by having investors take on additional risk. For considering the economic well-being of workers, it is incorrect financial analysis to consider a rate of return without considering the risk of the portfolio.

Many individuals hold a diversified portfolio in their retirement accounts, holding both stocks and bonds. For an individual holding both assets, the marginal dollar invested in each of these assets is of roughly the same value. Therefore, the composition of Social Security is not very important for these people. However, many individuals have no stocks and some have no bonds. For these people, the composition of Social Security investments is more important.

If an investor who preferred a diversified portfolio were required to hold a portfolio that was completely in stocks or completely in bonds, this would be a portfolio that was different from the portfolio the investor would have chosen. In that sense the investor would be made worse off with either of these restrictions, in an ex ante sense, even though the expected rate of return on the portfolio would go up if shifting to an all-stock portfolio and down if shifting to an all-bond portfolio. In contrast, a restriction on part of an investor's portfolio will be of little consequence to the investor when the rest of the investor's portfolio can be adjusted to offset the restriction. Many people have the ability to adjust balances in other retirement accounts to offset changes in the financial risks associated with Social Security. However, this option is not available to those with little financial wealth outside Social Security—roughly half the working-age population currently.[19]

How an individual should choose a combination of risk and return depends on the risk tolerance (risk aversion) of the investor along with other factors, such as other sources of financial risk. A similar analysis would hold for the choice of bonds from different suppliers—corporate bonds as opposed to Treasury bonds. Investment professionals and economic theory both suggest that most people should hold diversified portfolios, including both stocks and bonds. Some people, with well above average risk tolerance, should hold all stocks. Other people, who are very risk averse, should hold almost all bonds. Thus, a mandatory uniform portfolio for individuals that was completely in Treasury bonds would not be an optimal portfolio for the population as a whole. Recognizing that many people have little financial wealth and so cannot change the rest of their portfolio to offset a mandate, a mandatory uniform portfolio for individual accounts that was completely in Treasury bonds would not be an optimal portfolio for the population as a whole.

The lack of stockownership by many households provides one rationale for diversification of Social Security funds into stocks and corporate bonds. As with advance funding, diversification could occur either through individual accounts or through a central trust fund. If done through individual accounts, households would be given the option of investing in stocks or stock funds in their own accounts. This would allow non-stockholders to invest in stocks, an option many, but not all, would likely take advantage of. We discuss the relative merits of individual accounts versus central trust fund investment in the discussion of Question 3.

If individual accounts are adopted, the Panel thinks that individuals should be allowed to invest in stocks and corporate bonds.

Next we consider the portfolio choice if individual accounts are not adopted, and a central trust fund is built up.

2.2 Risks and Returns with Trust Fund Investment in Stocks and Corporate Bonds

In the next three sections, we consider Trust Fund investment policy solely in terms of the risk and return from a good portfolio, ignoring possible political interference in the choice of portfolio.[20] In section 2.5, we examine how political factors may decrease the quality of the portfolio held by the Trust Fund and how additional political factors might affect what investment policy is desirable.

Currently, by law, the Social Security Trust Fund is invested completely in Treasury bonds. While these pay the market rate of return, the Trust Fund does not receive any "risk premium" for bearing some of the risk from holding riskier assets.

From a narrow economic perspective, i.e., in terms of risk and return on the portfolio, Social Security is capable of bearing some portfolio risk. That is, Social Security beneficiaries and taxpayers are capable of bearing some risk that returns on the Trust Fund portfolio would be higher or lower than anticipated and that future legislation would have to adapt taxes and/or benefits to such changing circumstances. The importance of the portfolio choice reflects the fact that many people hold little financial wealth and no stocks, and so have no ability to adjust their personal portfolios; for those with the ability to adjust the rest of their portfolios, the makeup of the Trust Fund portfolio is of less importance.

*Just as is the case for individual and corporate pension invest-
ments, in terms solely of risk and return to Social Security covered
workers (that is, excluding consideration of social investing and
corporate governance issues), a Social Security Trust Fund portfolio consisting entirely of Treasury bonds does not represent an
optimal portfolio.*

Changing the portfolio changes expected returns and risk.
The changed portfolio outcomes are likely to affect future
benefits and taxes. To the extent that investment returns are
reflected in benefit adjustments, a defined benefit system
resembles a defined contribution system and the portfolio
should reflect the risk aversion of future beneficiaries. The
average worker is not likely to be so risk averse that a portfolio without stocks would be optimal. Insofar as investment
returns are reflected in payroll tax changes, part of the portfolio risk gets shifted forward to future workers, a form of
intergenerational risk-sharing that the market can not reproduce. For example, a stock market decline need not be fully
reflected in the benefits of workers invested in the market at
that moment, particularly those close to retirement; part of
the decline could be reflected in higher taxes for current and
future workers. From these considerations, an optimal portfolio, considering just risks and returns, would take on some
stock and corporate bond risk for the additional expected
return.

To spell out the effects of a change in portfolio policy
would require describing how congressional action would
be different as a consequence of the different levels of investment earnings coming from a different portfolio. For example, it might be specified that the Trust Fund would be
allowed to vary within some band (relative to expenditures)
without congressional action, with future benefits and taxes

changed when the Trust Fund gets outside the band. Adjust-ments could be legislated to be automatic or Congress could be left to respond, depending on the economic positions of different groups and political pressures. The Office of the Actuary, which currently reports on actuarial balance, would change its reporting to include new targets for the Trust Fund accumulation.

Diversifying the planned portfolio for Social Security would increase the expected rate of return on the Trust Fund. Thus it would improve the intermediate-cost actuari-al evaluation of Social Security that is based on expected returns. The high- and low-cost projections might change differently to reflect lower or higher possible stock returns, respectively. Of course, this improved evaluation comes with an increase in the risk on the Trust Fund portfolio.[21]

2.3 Money's Worth and Investment in Stocks

Analysts of proposals that include stocks in individual accounts or in the Trust Fund have noted that such portfolio diversification would increase the expected rate of return on the portfolios held. In turn, an increased expected return on a portfolio would increase the expected financial return from Social Security taxes, often referred to as money's worth. One measure of the money's worth of Social Security is the average implicit rate of return an age cohort of workers can expect to receive on their lifetime contribution to Social Security.[22] Money's worth calculations have been used to compare how different groups fare financially relative to each other under current Social Security rules and can be used for such comparisons in any single proposal. Money's worth calculations have also been used to compare how a given group fares under alternative systems.

However, consideration of the well-being of workers must go beyond the standard money's worth calculation when comparing policies, such as investment in stocks, that imply different risk characteristics for Social Security benefits. It is necessary to consider risk when making use of such calculations, whether considering portfolio diversification with or without individual accounts (Geanakoplos, Mitchell, and Zeldes, 1998b). One way of presenting risk is by reporting on statistical distributions of prospective outcomes that workers in different cohorts would face. For example, see Olsen, et al., 1998; and Goodfellow and Schieber, forthcoming. Another way of presenting risk is by reporting money's worth calculations using several interest rates, as was done by the 1994–1996 Advisory Council on Social Security.

As discussed above, for workers with sufficiently large and diversified portfolios of retirement savings outside Social Security, the portfolio structure of individual accounts would not be important since they could adjust the remainder of their portfolio to offset any changes in portfolios in individual accounts. For these workers, the standard money's worth calculation interpreted as measuring economic well-being shows an improvement from the portfolio diversification portion of a policy change when one is not present. For workers without the ability to fully offset changes in their individual account portfolios, allowing individual accounts to be invested in stocks would represent an improvement. The standard money's worth calculation would still overstate the utility gain to such workers since it would not include an accounting for the additional risk being taken on with choice of a riskier portfolio.

A similar issue arises with a change in Trust Fund portfolio policy. The similarity is that, because there is an increase in risk-bearing, the standard money's worth calculation overstates the utility gain to workers from Trust Fund investment in stocks. Two differences exist, however, between the analyses for individual accounts and for Trust fund investment. First, as described above, the government could spread a stock market gain or loss across individuals of different age cohorts by changing taxes or benefits on current and future workers, which would reduce the importance of the riskiness of Trust Fund investment (see, e.g., Bohn, 1997).[23] Second, with individual accounts, workers can choose whether and to what degree they hold stocks, thus [24] allowing those workers who do not value the added return and risk from the stock market to avoid it. To the extent that individuals do a good job of portfolio choice, this would also reduce the importance of risk considerations, on average, for individual accounts.

Overall, the important lesson is that some consideration of risk is needed in order to use money's worth statistics to evaluate the desirability of stock investments in either individual accounts or a central Trust Fund.

2.4 Effects on the Aggregate Economy of Trust Fund Investment in Stocks and Corporate Bonds

Without additional net revenue, investment in stocks and corporate bonds by the Trust Fund implies larger sales of Treasury bonds to the private economy than would be the case if the Trust Fund held only Treasury bonds. For example, if the Trust Fund purchases $1 billion in stocks in a year, then the Trust Fund holding of Treasury bonds will be $1 billion less than if the stocks had not been purchased. If the non-Social Security budget does not change, then the Treasury must borrow this $1 billion from someone else. Similarly, without additional net revenue, diverting some payroll tax revenues into individual accounts would leave less revenue flowing into the Trust Fund; thus, the value of stocks and bonds acquired by individual accounts would be matched initially by a decrease in the value of Treasury bonds held by the Trust Fund. In both cases, the public would end up holding more Treasury bonds and fewer stocks and corporate bonds outside of Social Security. That is, changing the holdings from bonds to stocks would be initially an "asset swap," although one that would have effects on the economy, just as an open market operation by the Fed has effects on the economy.

A shift in investment from Treasury bonds to stocks and corporate bonds without more advance funding would not thereby immediately increase national savings and so national income. This conclusion applies to a change in Trust Fund portfolio policy and to reforms that would place assets in individual accounts thereby decreasing the amount of Treasury bonds held by the Trust Fund.

An asset swap is different from an increase in advance funding which directly increases economic growth; possible gains to the aggregate economy could come from two sources. One is a possibly greater rate of savings of the higher expected rate of return within Social Security, and so higher national savings over time. The second is a possible improvement in risk bearing in the economy as a consequence of having more people share in the risky returns—those who have little savings and can not readily invest in stocks and future taxpayers to the extent that fluctuations in returns affect the level of taxes. The gain to the aggregate economy from changing the investment portfolio of Social Security is not as large as the full increase in the expected return on such investments.

To consider the direct effect on savings, we consider the case where the government changes its portfolio policy while leaving the rest of current policy unchanged. In this case, the additional expected returns on the portfolio are all saved until such time as Congress adjusts benefits. Some workers will adjust their overall private portfolio to preserve roughly the same level of risk and expected retirement income, thus offsetting the increased saving by the government. Those with little financial wealth, however, will adjust neither their saving nor their portfolio in response. Thus, overall, we would expect an increase in national savings, in expected value terms. While it is analytically convenient to consider a change in portfolio policy while leaving the rest of a reform package unchanged, this political outcome is unlikely. Full analysis of the effect of a change in portfolio policy on advance funding and national savings requires consideration of the impact on the rest of policy, particularly the impact on the target chosen for the ratio of the Trust Fund to annual expenditures.

To consider the effect of wider bearing of risk, we note first that many individuals hold few financial assets. They, as well as some who have significant financial holdings, have little or nothing invested in stocks, although they have considerable implicit wealth in the form of projected Social Security benefits (Mitchell and Moore, forthcoming). This implies that the change in both private and Social Security portfolios from Trust Fund portfolio diversification would not be a "wash." While the risk-return tradeoff may not be a gain for everyone, it is likely to be an improvement on average.

Social Security taxes and benefits are distributed more evenly across the population than personal wealth. The gain to workers covered by Social Security from a more diversified portfolio (with or without individual accounts) is of importance beyond any gains to the economy as a whole.

A consequence of bringing more people into the pool bearing investment risk would be a decrease in the "risk premium" for risky investments (Bohn, 1997). The economy would be likely to respond in a way that would increase future expected output because of the change in the mix of investments in response to a lower risk premium. The magnitude of such a response, however, is difficult to predict, depends on the government response to changed interest rates, and is likely to be small compared with the size of the asset swap. Therefore, the improved risk bearing and the accumulation of higher expected returns—sources of potentially improved functioning of the economy—are smaller effects for the economy as a whole than would be the effects of new investment resulting from decreased consumption.

Substituting stocks for Treasury bonds in the portfolio of either the Trust Fund or individual accounts is initially matched by the opposite portfolio change on the part of the public. Over time, the relationship is more complicated. Over time, the quantity of Treasury bonds held by the public depends on the level of outstanding public debt, less the part held in Social Security. Economic growth, congressional tax and spending decisions and Social Security holdings of Treasury bonds all affect how much Treasury debt is held by the public. Over time, the quantity of stocks and corporate bonds held by the public depend on the level of corporate investment, the extent of stock and bond financing of investment, and the holdings of stocks and corporate bonds within Social Security. The portfolio choice of Social Security and its degree of advance funding affect these later decisions by altering asset prices and future asset returns.

The Panel thinks that, taking into account only economic risk and returns from an optimal portfolio (that is, excluding consideration of social investing and corporate governance issues), the increase in expected returns from a well-diversified Trust Fund portfolio is sufficiently large that it is worth taking the additional risk.

2.5 Structural and Political Issues Associated with Private Investment

The possibility of a gain from Trust Fund portfolio diversification and its magnitude depend on the quality of portfolio investment decisions. Thus the following discussion addresses how such investment might be organized, and the extent to which this kind of administrative structure could both protect government portfolio choice from deviating from the optimal portfolio and protect corporate governance from undue federal interference.

Careful design of the governance institution for diversified investment is extremely important in order to shield fund accumulation, portfolio decisions and corporate governance from political pressures.

The Panel thinks that both the Federal Reserve Board and the Thrift Savings Plan (TSP) for federal employees provide useful models for the design of a possible Social Security Investment Board.

The Federal Reserve Board is in charge of monetary policy for the country. It has great independence in setting policy for the long-run benefit of the economy, insulated from short-run political pressures. Central to the Board's design is a process of Presidential nomination and Senate confirmation and overlapping 14-year terms, with no removal from office without cause. This institution has served the country well, and a similar structure would be desirable to govern Social Security investments.

Concerns about whether Social Security would invest wisely and whether Social Security ownership of shares of stock would affect corporate governance unduly are similar to concerns addressed in the creation of the TSP—the 401(k) system of defined contribution pensions created in 1986 for federal employees. The legislative history of the TSP reveals a strong consensus against political interference and against social investing. The authors of the plan carefully drafted the enacting legislation to protect against these threats, and to date these pitfalls have been avoided.

The institutional structure of the TSP includes the following features. By law, the TSP's investments in stocks are limited to index funds, defined as a "commonly recognized index" that is a "reasonably complete representation of the United States equity markets." In addition to selecting an index, the TSP Board selects a private fund manager through competitive bidding. The private manager, not the government, invests the funds and holds the voting rights on shares (indeed, the TSP Board is prohibited by law from exercising voting rights). Moreover, the fund manager has a strict fiduciary duty to manage the fund solely in the interest of its investors. Further protection is provided by commingling TSP funds with those of private investors using the same private fund manager. The TSP Board and its Executive Director are named fiduciaries. They must act prudently and solely in the interest of TSP participants and beneficiaries, and are subject to the requirements and provisions of the

Employee Retirement Income Security Act of 1974 (ERISA). TSP Board members do not serve "at the pleasure of the President" and cannot be removed by the President. They are required by law to have substantial expertise in pensions and investing. Neither Congress nor the Administration controls their budget. To date, there has been no political interference in the investment decisions of the Thrift Savings Plan for federal employees, reflecting, in part, the structure of its governance.

State pension plans for state employees have not generally been designed with all of the above safeguards. Their history includes some local preference investing, as well as some social investing, e.g., avoidance of investment in local companies operating in South Africa or in the tobacco industry. These actions have been the result of both direct legislation and pension board decisions. While highly visible, in the aggregate these deviations from investment concerned solely with risks and returns have not represented a large proportion of investment decisions. In addition, almost all state pension plans have placed the voting rights from their shares in the hands of private fund managers, who are motivated by both fiduciary obligations and their personal reputations to vote the shares in the interest of the covered workers and beneficiaries. However, a few public plans have been active in pressing policies affecting corporate governance.

There are concerns that Trust Fund investment or government-organized account investment in stocks might be used to affect corporate decisions in adverse ways. While ownership powers that are used to promote profitability are an appropriate use of ownership powers, use of powers for other purposes would be political interference. Allocating the voting rights to private fund managers who have a fiduciary duty to vote the shares solely in the economic interest of covered workers is an attempt to restrict these powers to appropriate uses. This is the route that TSP has gone. However, there is concern that with significant voting power, people with other causes in mind would be drawn to attempting to use these powers.

It is appropriate to be concerned about the efficacy of this insulation from political interference. On the one hand, activists would be drawn to use this power as another route into influence. On the other hand, corporations generally would oppose the use of these powers in any particular context as a precedent that they would fear. Congress does have other methods for accomplishing activists' goals, so activists will not necessarily pursue this method when other methods offer less political resistance. A central question is the extent to which the creation of insulation and of political precedents would result in a widely held perception that using Social Security for other than Social Security purposes would be politically dangerous to elected officials. This would depend on the extent to which the public would view the protection of Social Security from such approaches as important.

While the actuarial and economic implications of private investment by the Trust Fund are positive if sound investment policies are used, there is concern about political pressures that would interfere with good investment policies. In addition, there is concern that the government might use its ownership position to unduly influence corporate decisions.

The TSP represents an approach to stock and corporate bond investment that has worked at least on a small scale. Of course it is important to recognize that the scale of investment by Social Security would dwarf that of the TSP. In addition, under the TSP, plan assets are owned by plan participants, as would not be the case with direct Trust Fund investment.

Some analysts have expressed concern that investments in stocks—on the part of either the Trust Fund or individual accounts—would increase political sensitivities to the performance of capital markets, perhaps inappropriately influencing the functioning of other parts of the government, such as the setting of monetary and antitrust policies. While government is already concerned with the performance of capital markets, such concern might be heightened. With a widely diversified portfolio, however, investment in any single firm would not represent a large fraction of total investment. It is an open question whether the government's level of concern would become inappropriate to the financial interests of the American public.

Another concern related to the politics of Trust Fund investment in equities is that Congress might not do a good job of spreading the risk in the return across different age cohorts. In particular, Congress may be more prone to act quickly after good returns than after bad returns. A particular concern is that Congress may delay needed adjustments after there was good reason to think that the long-run rate of return had gone down.[24]

The Panel recognizes that either Trust Fund investment in stocks or government-organized individual accounts would be a new institution, making it difficult to predict exactly how the institution would work. It is appropriate to build design features in a new institution that would limit undesirable effects should they develop. Therefore, the Panel thinks that initial legislation should contain a cap on the fraction of ownership of any firm (through index fund ownership). A cap in the range of 5 to 10 percent seems suitable, although 5 to 10 percent is still a large share when it comes to corporate decision-making. Over time, the cap could be raised if these fears are not realized.[25]

If the Trust Fund invests in stocks and corporate bonds, the Panel recommends use of a governance structure similar to that of the Thrift Savings Plan (TSP). If there are individual accounts organized by the government, the Panel also recommends a governance structure similar to that of the TSP for investment management of such accounts, since a number of political issues are similar with both types of investment.[26] Initial legislation should contain a cap on the fraction of any firm owned through the index fund.

The Congress could create a Social Security Investment Board, structured similarly to the Federal Reserve Board, responsible for overseeing Trust Fund investments. Given the visibility that would result from the hearing process used to confirm appointments, it may be hoped that those appointed to the Board would bring considerable expertise and experience in both investment decisions and financial markets. While some issues would be addressed by legislation, others would be left to the Board as part of its charge. As investments increased, the Board would use multiple providers of index funds, pooling the returns if there were individual accounts so that returns to individuals would not depend on which investment manager was being used for a particular account. The Social Security Investment Board could be explicitly charged to inform the Congress and the public if any pending legislation would harm the financial status of the Trust Funds. While a structure parallel to that of the TSP could be developed, consideration should be given to building on the latter by commingling Social Security Trust Fund investment and TSP investments. Care would have to be taken to preserve the fiduciary obligations of the TSP Board to TSP investors while allowing the Board to provide services to Social Security. The actual investments could then be implemented by the TSP on behalf of the Social Security Investment Board. In this way, concerns of federal employees about their own retirement accounts might serve to alert the public about proposals that could affect Social Security.

Estimates of the fraction of stocks that would be held by Social Security depend on projections of the growth of the stock market, the amount of advance funding and the portion of advance fund that is legislated to be invested in stocks. Various estimates have been produced.[27] Given the difficulty of predicting future stock market growth and concern that Trust Fund holdings in the stock market might become too large, as discussed above, a cap could be legislated on the percentage of shares of any firm that are held by the Trust Fund. Chile has such a cap on the holdings of any mutual fund (AFP) holding Social Security accounts.

Another set of policy concerns relates to investments abroad. Some analysts have called for legislation that would exclude such investments from those allowed for the Trust Fund. Because such legislation would limit the available diversification, it would result in a deviation from strict concern with risks and returns. Since many American firms have considerable investments abroad, some international diversification could be attained without directly purchasing foreign stocks. The result would still be a portfolio with a lower expected return attainable at a given level of risk. Portfolio opportunities that remain, however, would still be better than with a portfolio of 100 percent Treasuries.

In considering the returns that might accrue to a government-selected portfolio, there are two benchmarks: (1) whether the portfolio would do better (adjusting for risk) than one invested 100 percent in Treasuries, as at present;

and (2) whether a government-selected portfolio would yield better net returns, accounting for risk, than the aggregate of investments that would be selected in individual accounts. The above discussion has focused on the former benchmark in considering the investment policy for a Trust Fund that might become large and sustained. The differences between Trust Fund and individual account investments are examined in the next section in the discussion of Question 3.

Even with a governance design similar to that of the Thrift Savings Plan there could well be some political interference in investment decisions and inappropriate influence on corporate governance. Nevertheless, the Panel thinks the Trust Fund would hold a better portfolio, even after adjusting for risk, with some investment in stocks and corporate bonds than with a portfolio invested solely in Treasury bonds. A dissenting view is that because of these political issues, it would be better to keep the Trust Fund solely invested in Treasury bonds.

If the Trust Fund is sustained as more than a contingency reserve, and if an investment management structure similar to that of the Thrift Savings Plan is employed, then the Panel recommends Trust Fund investment in stocks and corporate bonds provided that the Fund does not own more than 5 to 10 percent of the stock of any firm.

A dissenting view is that the Trust Fund should not invest in private securities. In this view, the relative magnitude of TSP stock holdings versus the potential holdings by the Social Security Trust Fund are so different that the comparison drawn here is inappropriate and the economic consequences of the political decision that would ensue from ownership of stock by a government-sponsored trust fund would be undesirable. Specifically this view holds that the traditional role of the federal government in the political structure of our society, in the regulation of business, and in the operations of our market economy would be affected if the Social Security Trust Fund should become the largest holder of private market capital in our economy. Based on these considerations, in this view, the optimal portfolio for a Social Security Trust Fund should continue to be 100 percent government bonds. Moreover, a dissenting view is that the accumulation of a substantial trust fund is a remote possibility rendering this recommendation moot.

The Panel recommendation recognizes that a very small investment in stocks would create more administrative burdens than would justify the gains to diversification. At the same time, the Panel recognizes that if the Trust Fund investment became too large, it might exercise too much influence on private markets and allocation decisions. An initial cap of 5 to 10 percent might be relaxed once we gain experience and learn about the impact of Trust Fund investments on corporate governance issues.

We have described the advantages of diversification if individual accounts are adopted or if, instead, a central Trust Fund were built up. There is dissent on the Panel about which of these methods for diversification is preferable. We discuss the choice between a central Trust Fund and individual accounts under the next question.

Question 3

Individual Accounts vs. Single Collective Fund

Should the reformed system create individual (funded defined-contribution) accounts, or should it remain a single collective fund with a defined-benefit formula?

In this section, we describe some of the advantages and disadvantages of creating a system of individual defined-contribution accounts relative to retaining a single collective fund with a defined-benefit formula. This involves a number of issues of economics, including administrative costs, as well as a number of normative and political concerns. We begin by considering the issue of administrative structure and costs.

3.1 Administrative Structure and Costs

There are many different ways in which individual accounts might be organized. We use the term *government-organized accounts* to denote individual account systems in which the government arranges for both the record keeping for the accounts and the investment management for the funds in the accounts—whether these functions are performed by government agencies or by private firms under contract to the government. An example of government-organized accounts is the federal employees' Thrift Savings Plan (TSP), a defined-contribution pension plan which contracts with a government agency to perform record keeping and with a private firm to do fund management. We use the term *privately organized accounts* to denote individual account systems in which individuals directly select private firms to do the record keeping and investment management. An example is individual retirement accounts (IRAs), where individuals select their own private financial institution.[28]

There are two types of structure needed under an individual accounts plan. First a structure is needed for accumulation in individual accounts. A second structure is needed for the provision of retirement income flows. In this section we consider costs for a government-organized system. For a privately organized system, we consider costs under Question 5.

The Panel recognizes that administrative costs are a significant issue and thinks that any reform with individual accounts needs to carefully calculate the added costs and compare these to any added benefits from individual accounts.

The costs of organizing the accounts depend on the organization of the accounts and on the level of services provided with the accounts. Examples of variation in the level of services include variations in the frequency of deposits of withheld funds into the accounts, the number of alternative investment options available, the frequency of interfund transfers that are allowed, the frequency of reporting on balances, the availability of information (e.g., an 800 number), the ease of communication (e.g., the presence of people who can speak different languages), the amount of education made available to workers. Different divisions of tasks among workers, employers, financial institutions and government may allocate these costs differently.

The Panel urges that all proposals to establish individual accounts spell out which aspects of collection, accumulation, asset management, and distribution would be done by the government, employers, asset management firms, and individuals. This will help assure that different cost estimates are comparable in that they are costing the same set of tasks.

To assist in this process, we provide in the following box a list of the tasks needed to implement individual accounts.[29] Some of these are one-time tasks or choices needed to set up the system. Others are tasks needed to be done repeatedly. We include a list of tasks for government organized accounts, and then show the additional tasks for privately organized accounts.

Tasks in Implementing Individual Accounts

This list first considers tasks in implementing government-organized accounts, and then notes tasks that would be different with privately organized accounts.

Government-Organized Accounts

This list assumes that contributions are received throughout the year, and are linked to individual tax payers after the end of the year, when W–2s are filed. It also assumes that the government receives the money, arranges for investment, recordkeeping and benefit payments. An asterisk (*) indicates tasks now done by the Social Security Administration or Treasury, or similar tasks. In some cases, the tasks become more complex because of differences in timing or other concerns.

---

1. Collect Contributions from Employers

a. Receive and record money from employers shortly after each payday.*

b. Reconcile amounts received with quarterly 941 and annual W–2 reports to detect missing or discrepant payments.*

c. Segregate account contributions from other taxes paid by employers.

2. Invest Funds

a. Select a private fund manager(s).

b. Invest new contributions during the year according to government policy.

c. Designate a default investment portfolio for individuals not selecting one.

d. Report investment returns to the recordkeeper—annual average for new contributions, monthly/quarterly for account balance valuations.

3. Credit Workers' Accounts with New Contributions

a. Find missing or inconsistent reports from employers by reconciling annual and quarterly reports and correspond with employers to fix it.*

b. Record new contributions to individual accounts. Identify discrepancies between W–2s and SSN files and correspond with employers or employees to fix mistakes.

c. Set up new information system of records needed to administer accounts: workers' ID, portfolio choice, effective date of choice, interfund transfers and date of interfund transfer, death beneficiary designation, marital status, spouse ID, and spousal consent code (depending on policy), current address.

4. Enroll Workers and Get Portfolio Choice (and Other New Information)

Depends on employer involvement (either mandatory or voluntary). Options include: (i) ongoing requirement that employers enroll new employees and report portfolio choices annually (on W–2s or W–4s); (ii) one-time employer responsibility to enroll workers in the plan and send data to the record keeper; (iii) do not involve employers—deal directly with workers through 1040s, correspondence, phone, website or in person.

5. Educate and Communicate with Workers

a. "Wholesale" tasks (such as in the TSP) include developing educational brochures, videos, training courses for employers to use to enroll workers.

b. "Retail" tasks (performed by employers in the TSP) include one-on-one communication with workers—via Social Security (or IRS?) field offices, an 800 number, website.

6. Pay Death Benefits

a. Determine policy for death benefits including registry of state laws on inheritance rights and rules for determining jurisdictions, if relevant.

b. Set rules of evidence for determining correct death beneficiary and maintain record system to support it.*

c. Resolve competing claims when they occur.*

7. Implement Policy on Treatment of Accounts at Divorce

Possible policies include: (i) let courts decide; (ii) automatically divide 50/50 changes in account balances that occurred during the marriage; and (iii) automatically divide contributions each year between spouses. Depending on policy, tasks include:

a. Set policy for treatment of QDRO (qualified domestic relations order from court).

b. Maintain historical records that can be used to retroactively combine and split two individuals' change in account balances for a period of years or each year, link accounts of husbands and wives and transact a split.

c. Set up systems for verifying marital status and spouse ID, and policies for resolving disputes, discrepancies, and informing each party of transactions made on their accounts.

8. Pay Retirement Benefits

a. Determine policies about nature of withdrawal options.

b. With annuities, determine whether government or insurance companies will: (i) assume mortality and investment risk; and/or (ii) administer the annuities.

c. If insurance companies, determine policy for their involvement—e.g., standards for participation, competitive bidding for group contract, some sort of reinsurance.

d. Policy on joint-and-survivor annuities and beneficiary designation for non-annuitized funds (or period certain annuities).

9. Retirement Benefit Counseling (assuming a number of withdrawal options are available)

a. Explain to retirees what the choices are and what terms mean and run scenarios of how different choices would affect the particular retiree and spouse.

b. Set policies (if any) on who will provide the information and who will pay for it.

10. Early Access (if loans or withdrawals end up being allowed for "hardship.")

a. Determine hardship rules and how they will be applied.

b. If loans, set up systems for how they will be repaid.

Privately Organized Accounts: Additional Tasks

This list assumes that funds are withheld and paid by employers to the government (as they are now) and that employers report annually on W–2s the amounts belonging to each worker. The government's tasks in collecting contributions would be the same as in government organized accounts.

When W–2s are in, the government would send each worker's funds to a financial institution chosen by the worker. The financial institution would be responsible for all further dealing with the account holder. It would be responsible for: investing funds, crediting workers accounts with new contributions, getting information about the worker's portfolio choice and other data needed to pay benefit to the worker or his/her beneficiaries, educate and communicate with workers about investment choices, pay death benefits, implement policy on treatment of divorce, pay retirement benefits under applicable rules, and provide retirement benefit counseling. It would also be responsible for enforcing whatever policy applies with regard to early access.

New issues and tasks that arise under this model:

a. Government would maintain a default plan or default institution for workers who fail to designate a financial institution.

b. Government would set rules on financial institutions eligible to hold Social Security accounts.*

c. If workers would be required to hold their funds in only one institution at a time, government and financial institutions would put systems in place to ensure that happened.

d. Once money is sent to the financial institution, it would be responsible for receiving portfolio choices from workers, sorting out mistakes and making employees whole under whatever rules apply.

e. Government policies might regulate fee arrangements of financial institutions, terms on which accounts are accepted by institutions, and possibly, marketing practices.

f. Government policies might regulate allowable portfolios.

g. Government would monitor institutions' compliance with whatever rules apply to the accumulation and distribution of account funds.*

h. Auditing, trustee, legal and related functions, to the extent not included above.

Moving to a system of individual Social Security accounts would considerably expand the number of such type of accounts in existence. To put the scope of a possible new system in perspective, the TSP maintains fewer than 3 million individual accounts; the largest number of existing individual accounts handled by a firm has under 6 million accounts; and there are fewer than 10 million IRAs with multiple investment options. No one has an existing system that currently handles the administrative complexities of a program with more than 140 million accounts, as would happen with individual accounts. Creating an administrative system for that number of accounts would take time and resources.[30,31]

Measuring Costs

Setting up and administering a system of individual accounts involves a variety of types of costs. Some would be one-time costs to set up the system, independent of the size of the system. Other setup costs would depend on the number of participants. In terms of ongoing costs, most are fixed costs per account, while some depend on the size of the account. Since the bulk of ongoing costs would likely be fixed costs per account, we present estimates in those terms (for example, x dollars per account per year). It may be useful for some purposes, however, to express these costs in other ways. One familiar method of stating costs is as an annual management fee in percentage terms (for example, y percent of the accumulated balance in the account per year). Once the size of the accounts has been estimated, a dollar cost per year and a percentage of balances per year can be related by calculations that equate the present discounted value of costs over the career of a worker. If charges are imposed to cover the costs under these two methods, the charges will be equal on a lifetime basis, but will likely differ under the two methods in any given year or stage of life. With balances that grow relative to wages, a constant percentage of balances is a smaller charge in early years and a larger charge in later years. A third way to report on the costs is in terms of the percentage decrease in the accumulation in an account at retirement age as a consequence of the administrative charges, called the *charge ratio*.

We begin by considering government-organized accounts that have relatively low costs and provide a relatively low level of services. Under question 5 we consider the added costs and of moving to privately organized accounts.

3.2 An Illustrative Low-Cost/Low-Services Plan

Currently, Social Security costs about $18 per person (workers and beneficiaries) per year. Excluding the costs of the disability program, OASI costs about $11 per person per year. The estimate for Social Security is based on 1997 administrative cost of $3.4 billion for the total program divided by 191 million participants (147 million workers and 44 million beneficiaries). The cost for only the retirement and survivors part of Social Security is based on administrative cost of $2.1 billion.[32] The total cost of OASI divided by the number of workers is a cost of $14 per worker.

Almost all proposals with individual accounts envision continuing with some defined benefit retirement system as well as continuing disability and young survivor benefits using the current administrative structure. Therefore, the lowest-cost method of designing individual accounts would use government-organized accounts and would build as much as possible on the existing Social Security structure.

Transmission of Funds

At present, employers pay Social Security taxes to the Treasury shortly after each pay period, with a frequency depending on the size of the employer. However, these payments are not individually identified to the Treasury; that is, the Treasury knows the employer but not the individual employee associated with any tax payment. Once a year, employers file W–2 forms that show the annual taxable earnings of individual workers, which are needed for the eventual determination of benefits. Until 1978, firms reported on individual earnings quarterly, but that frequency was reduced to hold down costs, particularly for employers with few workers. At present, of the 6.5 million employers that report to the Social Security Administration each year, 5.4 million file their W–2 reports on paper; these include more than 4 million employers with 10 or fewer employees.

While shifting to more frequent reporting might not be costly for employers with electronic record keeping, doing so would represent a significant cost for small businesses. Therefore, in the low-cost/low-services version of individual accounts, we assume that these taxpaying and reporting practices of private firms would not change. With this structure, the Treasury could place the portion of aggregate payroll tax revenues that was allocated for individual accounts in a separate trust fund, which would earn interest. Such a fund could hold Treasury debt, but it might be better to hold the estimated average portfolio, based on existing allocations and previous earnings. This would permit an allocation to individual accounts that reflected individual portfolio choices (which would be made before the year began). Without a direct adjustment, there would be some difference between the total investment returns of the separate trust fund and the amounts to be credited to individual accounts. This difference could be averaged over time, or allocations could be adjusted each year. However, the allocation could not recognize the actual timing of payments by different workers; all workers would be treated as if the timing of their withheld tax payments were the same as the timing of aggregate withholdings.

Once a year, the Treasury would allocate the accumulated separate trust fund to individual accounts. To process almost all of the accounts without greater cost than at present would probably require at least 6 months after the end of the year in which the taxes had been collected. More time would be required for those cases in which there was a mismatch between the reported W–2 information and Social Security records, as well as for the self-employed, who can file as late as April 15 (and later if they file for an extension). In a system this large, even a small percentage of errors adds up to large number of errors. Currently, roughly 3 percent of W–2 forms (6 million cases) require direct contact with employer or employee to match the W–2 and Social Security records. With the additional element of portfolio allocation, more errors would have to be resolved.

Portfolio Choice

Under this structure, individuals would inform Social Security about the division of their deposits among the available portfolios. Workers might do this directly or through their employers, but in either case it would have to be done before the start of the calendar year, with the allocation unchanged from the previous year unless the worker requested otherwise. Some individuals, particularly newly covered workers, would not have selected an allocation, and there would have to be a default portfolio for these workers. This could be legislated to be similar to the current portfolio of the Social Security Trust Fund, or the average portfolio in individual accounts, or a prudently selected portfolio. In addition to directing the flow of new deposits among different index funds, workers would be allowed to shift existing account balances on a limited basis, such as once a year. Similarly, information on the level of their accounts would be provided directly to workers only once a year. Workers could infer the value of their accounts by knowing the number of units held in each account and checking the values of those units, which would likely be presented regularly in the media.

To keep costs low, worker education about portfolio choices would be limited to providing pamphlets on investment strategy. It should be noted, however, that experience with worker education in 401(k) plans shows that considerably more substantial (and expensive) worker education is needed to have a noticeable effect on workers' investment choices (Bayer, Bernheim, and Scholz, 1996). In addition to this minimal outreach providing education, Social Security would need to respond to questions asked by covered workers.

Handling and managing the aggregate funds would probably require only a small management fee. Currently, the TSP is charged roughly 1 basis point by the fund managers handling the bond and stock funds.

The cost of paying retirement benefits from individual accounts must also be considered. Assuming annuitization were mandated, the least-cost approach would be automatic annuitization of these funds according to rules set by legislation, with the payments added to the payment of whatever defined benefits were maintained. Information would be provided to beneficiaries on the source of each payment.

We cannot be sure what it would cost to add such a low-cost/low-services system to existing Social Security administration. A starting place for considering these administrative costs is the portion of the costs of the TSP that fall on the TSP (that is, excluding the costs that fall on federal agencies that educate workers, answer questions and report earnings records to the TSP and excluding the administrative costs coming from the payment of annuities (which are paid by retirees and reflected in the price of annuities). The TSP cost is currently roughly $20 per worker per year, although the costs were lower when fewer services were provided.[33] With 140 million accounts, a cost of $20 per worker would be an aggregate cost of $2.8 billion per year.

There are a number of issues involved in comparing TSP costs with the incremental costs of the low-cost/low-services system just described. On the one hand, the TSP provides better services (in frequency of reporting, frequency of portfolio change, and frequency of deposit), must deal with loans against workers' accounts, and has fewer economies of scale. In addition, there may be some economies of scope. For example, a single annual statement can contain information on both parts of the system. These factors tend to lower the costs of Social Security individual accounts relative to TSP costs. On the other hand, there are factors that tend to raise the cost of Social Security individual accounts relative to TSP costs. First, many costs of the TSP system are borne by federal agencies as employers. They handle the education of participants (although provide more education than described in the low cost plan), respond to their questions, enroll them in the plan, transmit their portfolio choices electronically, and make employees whole when reporting errors cause them to lose investment returns on their contributions. If employers do not fill the roles they fill with the

TSP, these costs will likely fall on Social Security. Many of the 140 million workers have more limited education and less proficiency in English than is typical of federal employees, and direct contact would be needed to handle the tasks above. Second, Social Security covers many small employers that report Social Security records on paper, rather than electronically, which would add to the cost and risk of errors in record keeping. Third, Social Security covers part-time, intermittent, and highly mobile workers, many of whom have multiple employers, whereas federal employees have low labor mobility. Fourth, there are likely to be mandatory adjustments upon divorce. Finally, there will be costs of providing benefits, whether annuitized or paid out regularly, which are not part of TSP costs. While we can not be sure what such a system would cost, the range of $25-$50 per worker per year is a rough order of magnitude for a low cost/low services plan.[34,35]

While the bulk of the costs would be fixed per account, their effect on the accumulation in individual accounts would depend on how charges for these costs were allocated across accounts of different sizes. The charges could be proportional to deposits or to account sizes, implying that all workers with the same portfolio choice would receive the same rate of return. Alternatively, the charges could include a fixed component reflecting the underlying structure of the costs, implying that workers with higher accumulations would have better rates of return net of charges. Presumably, government-organized accounts would follow the former approach.

How would these added costs affect the retirement income of covered workers? The relative significance of a cost range of $25-$50 per worker per year would depend on the proportion of workers' earnings being deposited in the accounts and the size of their earnings. In 1996, 22 percent of workers covered by Social Security earned less than $5,000, while 58 percent earned below $20,000 (Table 1). In 1997, mean Social Security taxable earnings were approximately $23,000. If 1.6 percent of workers' earnings went to individual accounts, a $25–$50 cost charged to the account would be equal to 7–14 percent of the new contribution (equivalent to a "front load" charge) for the mean earner; with 2 percent accounts, the front load would be 5–11 percent; with 5 percent accounts, it would be 2–4 percent; and with 10 percent accounts, it would be 1–2 percent. These calculations would be the same for workers at any earnings level if charges were the same percentage for all workers. If charges reflected

Table 1

Percent of Workers with Social Security Earnings Below Specified Levels
Wage and Salary Workers, 1996

Workers		
Number	Percent	With annual taxable earnings of less than:
29,554	22	$ 5,000
46,438	35	10,000
61,816	46	15,000
76,178	58	20,000
88,900	67	25,000
99,458	73	30,000
114,629	85	40,000
123,641	91	50,000
128,591	95	60,000
129,578	96	63,000
136,689	100	63,001

Source: Office of the Actuary, SSA.

some of the fixed costs of accounts, the load would be larger for low earners and smaller for high earners. Another way to describe these charges is to ask what charge as a fraction of assets under management would cover these costs on a lifetime basis, assuming that the cost grew with average wages. With 2 percent accounts an annual $25–$50 change would be equivalent to a 25–50 basis point charge on assets under management over a 40-year career; with 5 percent accounts roughly equivalent to a 10–20 basis point charge.

We note that the distribution of earning of workers covered by Social Security is very different from that of earnings of current 401(k) participants. In contrast to Table 1, of workers participating in 401(k) plans in 1993, only about 20 percent earned less than $20,000 (EBRI, 1994).

We cannot be sure what a low-cost/low-services system of government-organized individual accounts would cost or what services would be legislated. If the costs were the same as for the Thrift Savings Plan, the government's administrative costs of the reformed system would more than double current Social Security administrative costs, which were $16 per participant in 1997. As discussed above, costs of a low cost/low services system will likely be higher than TSP costs.

Because of higher administrative costs associated with individual accounts the implicit rate of return on Social Security with individual accounts would be lower than the return that could be achieved without individual accounts if the Social Security Trust Fund were invested and maintained in a similar portfolio. This cost needs to be balanced against any benefits of individual accounts considered in the following sections.

Costs would be raised by the provision of additional services, such as more frequent reporting on accounts, more frequent deposits into accounts, more frequently allowed real-locations of existing portfolios, more readily available information on account balance, or more worker education. Privately organized accounts would provide more services and a wider choice of investments, but at a higher cost. We discuss privately organized accounts further in Question 5.

3.3 Economics of Accumulation

In this section, we examine the economic differences and similarities between individual accounts and the current defined benefit system that occur in the accumulation phase.

Increased Advance Funding

These economic effects of an increase in advance funding would be similar whether the system has individual accounts or not (as discussed above under Questions 1 and 2), although the politics would differ (as is discussed below). With increased advance funding, future cohorts of workers could receive a higher implicit rate of return from Social Security with or without individual accounts. Over time, the amount of accumulation depends on the net rate of return, which depends on both portfolio choice and administrative charges and may be different with and without individual accounts.

Distribution of Risk

With individual accounts, the monthly benefits received because of a worker's account are determined by the value of the accumulation in the account at retirement and the terms on which annuities are available (assuming annuitization).

Thus workers directly bear the risk due to the market returns on the assets held in the account, and the risk about the terms on which annuities are available.[36]

If the Trust Fund holds a similar level of investment in a similar portfolio as the individual accounts, and if the government altered benefit levels to completely reflect investment returns, then the risk from market investment would be the same as with individual accounts. This means that the benefit levels of individuals in different cohorts would vary due to different realized market returns. However, under the defined-benefit approach, market fluctuations need not be fully reflected in the benefits of current workers since they could also be reflected in taxes or benefits of future workers. This provides the opportunity, not present in an individual account system, to spread the risk more broadly and evenly across age cohorts. Of course, the benefit of this possibility depends on how Congress responds to market returns that are different from projections; that is, how well Congress would spread the risks.[37]

In addition to risks in the rate of return while accumulating, there are risks in the terms on which annuities are available, since annuity pricing depends on both mortality projections and interest rates. The private market would decrease the level of annuitized monthly benefits paid from individual accounts in response to an increase in life expectancy, while the response of a defined benefit system (without automatic adjustment) would wait until Congress acted. This issue is discussed further in section 3.6. The analysis of the risk in the return while accumulating and the interest rate risk in the pricing of annuities need to be considered together, since optimal portfolio policy would recognize future annuitization as part of the modeling of total risk. Consideration of these risks for workers would need to reflect estimates of the choices workers would actually make. For more discussion of annuitization see section 5.3.

One of the potential advantages of individual accounts is that different workers could choose to hold different portfolios at any point in time, and that workers could vary their portfolios across time as they saw fit. For example, workers who were very risk averse or who faced other risks correlated with the stock market could choose to hold a portfolio with little or no equities, while workers who were less risk averse could choose a portfolio with substantially more in equities. This would enable risk to be spread more efficiently in the economy, as it would enable those most capable of or less averse to bearing risk to bear more of it. The gains from this variation in portfolios would depend on the extent to which people were successful in selecting portfolios suitable for their degree of risk aversion.[38] Also, individual accounts might not face the same level of restrictions on the choice of assets or the degree of stock market investment faced, for reasons of corporate governance, by the Trust Fund. This would result in a lower level of risk, for a given return, with individual accounts. For workers who make wise choices, these gains could be substantial. On the other hand, for individuals who make poor portfolio choices, individual choice may not be a benefit, but a cost. Currently, many workers have poor understanding of the workings of financial markets. To some extent, this would improve with individual accounts.

Risks associated with market fluctuations are present both in individual accounts and a defined benefit approach with the Trust Fund invested in equities. There are some differences, however. Individual accounts can improve the efficiency of risk bearing by allowing those who least want to bear risk to bear less of it. A defined-benefit approach can improve the efficiency of risk bearing by spreading risk across age cohorts.

Returns to different cohorts will differ from each other both in a defined benefit and defined contribution system. In a defined benefit system, the benefit formula and/or the tax rates will have to be adjusted at various times. This can create political pressures. With an individual account system, returns will differ due to different market experiences. Historically, the accumulations resulting from the same annual contributions and the same portfolio choice have varied widely as has the pricing of annuities. These variations are due to the outcome of market process, however, rather than being under political control. Even so, such variation is considered undesirable by some analysts and may generate a legislative response. For example, while there was no legislated response, there was considerable political pressure by "notch-babies" in response to the 1977 legislation that changed the benefit formula to correct a problem in the formula that had been enacted in 1972.

Money's Worth

One of the most popular arguments put forward in favor of individual accounts is that moving to a system of individual accounts would raise the rate of return on Social Security for all. The typical approach compares the historical rate or return on U.S. capital markets to the projected rate of return on Social Security, observes that Social Security returns are much lower, and then concludes that a shift to individual accounts would enable all households to attain the higher rates of return attainable on U.S. capital markets.

In section 2.3 we discussed why comparing expected rates of return on assets of programs with different degrees of risk (whether it be individual accounts invested in stocks or Trust Fund investment in stocks) did not give a good picture of worker well-being since it did not reflect risk considerations. Here we point out another difficulty with the popular argument, related to the transition costs of shifting to an individual account system.

Money's worth calculations for today's young workers show implicit rates of return that are below those for earlier cohorts. A decline in the rate of return since the early cohorts covered by Social Security is an inevitable result of having instituted a pay-as-you-go system.

Money's worth implicit rates for today's young workers are also below expected market rates of return. However, comparing a market return on a portfolio with a return on taxes is comparing apples and oranges. Comparing a benefit that could be financed by saving all of payroll taxes with projected Social Security benefits is similarly misleading. Proper comparisons of how a shift to individual accounts would affect projected money's worth are more complex than simply calculating the expected return on asset portfolios that might be held in individual accounts.

First, the existing system provides both life insurance in the event of early death of a worker and disability insurance and retirement benefits for previously disabled workers. Preserving these important functions would use part of payroll tax revenue. Keeping these benefits at their current levels would cost approximately 3 percent of taxable payroll during the next 75 years, more than the current cost of 2.4 percent. As part of overall reform, the level of these benefits can be changed. However, this should not be done as an accidental byproduct of reform of the retirement benefit system but rather as a result of an explicit examination of the workings of the disability and young survivor system.

Second, if the current Social Security system were to be fully replaced, it would be necessary to recognize the large unfunded obligation of Social Security. That is, some portion of current and future Social Security revenues, or some other revenue source, is needed to pay benefits to those already retired and those who will retire during any transition to a different system. This cost cannot be avoided if the expectations of retirees and those nearing retirement are to be met. The present value of future benefits already accrued based on past contributions (plan-termination unfunded accrued obligation, or "maximum transition cost") is about $9 trillion more than the current value of the Trust Fund (Goss, forthcoming). That is, $9 trillion plus the current value of the Trust Fund would be needed if Social Security were to stop collecting taxes and were to continue paying benefits based on current legislation and the history of earnings to date that have been subjected to tax.

Most proposals envision continuing with some defined retirement benefits that are not fully funded. Such proposals do not need to recognize all of the unfunded obligations. Indeed, Social Security can continue indefinitely without paying off its unfunded obligation. Over time, the size of the unfunded obligations may change, depending on taxes and benefits. To prevent this obligation from growing relative to the size of the economy, approximately 3 percent of payroll would be needed on an annual basis (Geanakoplos, Mitchell, and Zeldes, 1998a and b). More revenue would be needed to reduce unfunded obligations.

This plan-termination unfunded accrued obligation (maximum transition cost) is different from the present value of the actuarial imbalance, estimated to be about $3 trillion, which includes all benefits to be paid and taxes to be collected over the next 75 years for the ongoing program. A reform that restores actuarial balance must have a net change in benefits, taxes, and other revenue sources to cover the $3 trillion. A reform that also wanted to increase advance funding would need more resources.

Neither the unfunded obligation nor the costs of financing it go away by diverting revenue from the defined-benefit part of Social Security to individual accounts. These costs need to be paid even if a switch is made to an individual account system. If all of the cost of the unfunded obligation were allocated to individual accounts, it would completely eliminate the rate of return advantage of individual accounts. If all of the cost of the unfunded obligation were allocated to the defined benefit portion of a two-tier system, as in the typical proposal, the public could mistakenly believe that the returns on individual accounts are higher than on the defined benefit system, even when they are not. This misunderstanding could have political ramifications. To mitigate this effect, the costs remaining from underfunding could be divided between the defined-benefit and defined-contribution systems. Alternatively, these costs could be removed completely from Social Security and a separate revenue source developed to finance them.

Reducing the unfunded obligations by increasing advance funding does raise future implicit rates of return, while lowering the implicit rates of return from Social Security of workers who are financing the increase in advance funding.

It is important to distinguish between the rate of return on the portfolio held by the Trust Fund or in individual accounts and the implicit rate of return on Social Security taxes. The latter needs to recognize that part of payroll tax payments finance disability and survivors insurance, and part is used to finance the unfunded obligation. This conclusion holds with or without individual accounts.

More advance funding going into individual accounts or the Social Security Trust Fund would improve standard money's worth calculations for future workers, but would worsen it for cohorts that would finance the increase in advance funding.

With similar levels of unfunded obligation, money's worth with and without individual accounts will differ depending on differences in the net rates of return on the different portfolios, relative to differences in risk bearing. A full evaluation of returns and risks also needs to consider the insurance aspects of Social Security and the political risks, which are discussed below.

3.4 Benefit Structure

Much of the discussion of individual accounts has focused on the accumulation of resources within the accounts. There has been little public discussion of how the accumulations will be converted into retirement benefit flows and how an individual account system will be integrated with both disability benefits and survivor benefits for children who lose a parent. In our presentation of a low cost/low service system, we assumed that annuitization would be done by Social Security. Below, we consider private provision of annuities to workers. Here, we consider aspects of the benefit structure, continuing the assumption that benefits are provided by the government. The importance of the issues we discuss varies with the size of the individual accounts.[39,40]

Disability and Young Survivor Benefits

Since young disabled workers will not have had the opportunity to accumulate a sufficient account to finance disability needs, there is a need to provide disability benefits as insurance even with individual accounts. Some disabled workers survive until retirement age, as do many of their surviving spouses. Thus there is a need to integrate disability and retirement benefits, an integration that is more complicated and difficult with individual accounts than with a fully defined-benefit system. That is, the adjustment of defined benefits that would roughly match the value of funds in an individual accounts varies greatly with the age at which a worker becomes disabled or dies. Any adjustment will be uneven.[41]

Currently, the same benefit formula is used for disability and young survivor benefits as is used for retirement benefits. Some proposals preserve this structure. Thus, when proposals decrease retirement benefits in step with diverting revenues into individual accounts, they also decrease disability and young survivor benefits. Yet there is less time for accumulation in an individual account until the date of disability or early death than until the retirement age. Therefore, such an approach reduces available resources for the disabled and young survivors relative to those for retirees. Given the needs of the disabled and young survivors, it is not clear that such a reduction in relative benefits is warranted. At a minimum, the effect of such reforms on these groups needs to be carefully assessed.

Currently, Social Security provides disability benefits as well as retirement benefits for previously disabled workers and their surviving spouses. It also provides benefits for minor children in the event of the death of a parent. Introduction of individual accounts needs to be carefully integrated with both disability benefits and benefits for children after the death of a parent. Any change in the level of these benefits should not happen as an accidental byproduct of reform of the retirement benefit system, but should only be considered with an explicit examination of the workings of the disability and young survivor systems.

Divorce

At present, divorced spouses and divorced surviving spouses can receive benefits based on the earnings records of their former spouses, provided they were married at least 10 years. Even so, the poverty rate among elderly divorced women is very high (Grad, 1998). An individual account system can not easily replicate the current effect of divorce on benefits, although it is not clear that reproducing this pattern would be the most suitable outcome.

One approach to providing some protection from the economic consequences of divorce with individual accounts would be to have equal division of the portion of individual accounts of husbands and wives that are accumulated during marriage. This might be mandated or might be available as part of a divorce settlement. This approach would add to administrative costs, given the need to identify the amounts to be transferred, as well as which accounts to change. The added costs would be less if individuals were restricted to accounts with one institution than if individuals were allowed to have accounts at multiple financial institutions.

An alternative approach would be annual division of the contributions of husbands and wives to their individual accounts. This would remove the complication of adjusting accounts upon divorce, but would involve a considerable increase in record keeping. In addition to the need to track marriage and divorce, it would add to the names and Social Security numbers that would have to be handled as part of the allocation to accounts. This issue is discussed further below under the more general issue of the provision of retirement benefits to couples.

While the above two approaches to benefits after divorce address the accumulation in individual accounts during a marriage, they do not reflect future increases in Social Security benefits due to higher earnings resulting from the human capital built up during the marriage. An example is one spouse supporting the other while he or she is pursuing graduate education. No simple uniform rule for handling divorce will fit all diverse patterns that occur.

Currently, Social Security provides benefits to aged divorced spouses of retired workers and aged surviving divorced spouses based on lifetime earnings of the former spouse. Divorced women are among the poorest of the elderly. Introduction of individual accounts must consider carefully the rules governing disposition of the accounts in the event of a divorce and the effect on elderly unmarried divorcees.

Widowed Spouses

The poverty rate among elderly widows is roughly four times that among elderly couples, and many women who become widows experience a sharp decline in their ratio of income to needs (Grad, 1998; Holden, 1998). Currently, Social Security benefits are paid as an annuity, adjusted annually for cost-of-living increases. Widows are protected by being able to claim the larger of their own worker benefit or a survivor benefit based on the deceased spouse's record.

Indeed, many analysts have called for greater protection of widows within the current Social Security structure.

Currently, Social Security provides benefits to aged surviving spouses. On average, elderly widows and widowers are considerably less well-off than elderly couples. Introduction of individual accounts must consider carefully the effect on elderly surviving spouses.

The Panel thinks protection of a lower-earning spouse is important and needs to be addressed in any reform proposal. If a system does not mandate considerable benefits for a divorced or surviving spouse, at least it should have a division of accounts between spouses in some form.

Early division of accounts between spouses (for example, equal sharing of earnings annually) would not reproduce the current pattern of benefits of spouses, nor the patterns of benefits across couples with different relative earnings, nor the differences in benefits of single people and married couples. Reproducing that pattern using transfers among accounts would be difficult, and may not be desired. The desirability of the current structure has been controversial, with various previous Panels unable to agree on a system that is clearly better than the current structure.[42]

Low Earners

Currently Social Security uses a progressive benefit formula to provide a higher replacement rate for workers with low lifetime earners. This protects workers with low earnings throughout their careers, and also provides some insurance for everyone against a sustained drop in earnings at some point in a worker's career. Approaches to preserving this aspect of Social Security vary with the size of individual accounts relative to the overall size of the Social Security program. Proposals for individual accounts range from 1.6 percent of taxable payroll to 12.4 percent. However, expected retirement benefits from individual accounts are a larger fraction of total benefits than their share of total tax payments because of disability and young survivors benefits and the financing of the unfunded obligation. This needs to be kept in mind when assessing the steps needed to preserve protection of low earners.

Different proposals include different mechanisms for preserving part or all of the current provision for adequate retirement incomes that is reflected in higher benefits relative to contributions for low earners. For example, the Individual Account plan of the Advisory Council on Social Security makes the remaining defined-benefit portion of Social Security more progressive; the Advisory Council's Personal Security Account plan has two tiers, with a flat benefit that is the same for all full-career workers; the proposal by Kotlikoff and Sachs includes annual additions to accounts of low earners; and some analysts have called for increasing the benefits provided by the Supplemental Security Income (SSI) program to protect those with small accounts. In fact, the provision of a minimum income level for the elderly through some mechanism is a feature of almost all proposals, although proposals differ in the size of the minimum income level and the extent of attention to the adequacy of retirement incomes above such a minimum. Thus income adequacy may be preserved through a progressive defined-benefit formula in some form, with the degree of progressivity increased to reflect the removal of the defined-contribution portion (which by its nature is linear or regressive if charges to accounts include a fixed component without government matching). Alternatively, if no defined-benefit system remains, income adequacy concerns can be met by adding to the accounts of low earners, perhaps with a matching provision. This match could take a variety of forms, including adding an amount to the accounts of active workers that might be constant or might vary with earnings, perhaps similarly to the way the Earned Income Tax Credit varies with earnings. It could add to the contributions of low earners in each year or add to the accounts of workers with low accounts who reach retirement age. Any of these approaches would affect labor market incentives.[43]

The latter approach would also affect the incentive to take portfolio risks. Alternatively, the matching could depend on the earnings or accumulation of couples rather than individuals. This would improve the risk-sharing properties of the system, although they would be more complicated to administer than just considering individual workers.[44,45]

The Panel thinks that income redistribution to low income workers to increase their replacement rates is an important aspect of Social Security. If a combined system does not sufficiently preserve the redistributive characteristics of the program, it should include additional contributions to individual accounts of low earners.

3.5 Individual Values

The distinction between direct individual risk bearing and collective allocation of risk among workers and beneficiaries leads to a central issue of the values underlying the system.

The Panel recognizes that the choice between individual accounts and a fully defined-benefit system depends on more than actuarial and economic outcomes. Individual values play a role as well, since this choice involves a tension between a principle of individual responsibility, ownership and choice and a competing principle of collective responsibility that involves the sharing of costs and risks.

The tension between these two principles is present in many arenas of government policy, and a compromise between them frequently characterizes policy design. In the area of retirement income, this compromise is represented by having both private pensions and individual savings in addition to Social Security. Individual account proposals are also compromises between the two principles: some proposals preserve a defined-benefit component, and all envision a social safety net. Nevertheless, moving to individual accounts would result in a different balance between these two principles than is presently the case. That change in balance, in turn, could lead to additional shifts in the balance—in either the same or a reverse direction—based on the experience with a new institution. Indeed, such implications are one of the central issues in the debate about creating individual accounts.

3.6 Political Concerns

We have analyzed the economic implications of using a (partially) defined-contribution as opposed to (fully) defined-benefit approach to Social Security. We turn to the relationship between these approaches to reform and possible political outcomes.

Legislation actually adopted is likely to be a political compromise that differs from any single proposal put forth. Thus analysis needs to consider what Congress is likely to legislate. In addition, there is concern about future legislation. Concern about future legislation is usefully considered in three different ways. First, economic and demographic changes are likely to differ from whatever is projected when legislation is passed. Both the likelihood of new legislation and the nature of that legislation in response to deviations from projections are likely to be different with than without individual accounts. Second, individual accounts may alter the frequency and degree to which future taxes and benefits are changed in response to changes in the balance of political pressures. Third, the Social Security institutions themselves are likely to generate political pressures which may lead to changes in Social Security. Indeed, some political approaches may not be viable in the sense that their legislation generates political pressures which, in time, will defeat the primary purpose behind the initial legislation.

Increased advance funding, diversification into stocks and corporate bonds, and the creation of individual accounts are each likely to introduce different political pressures, and there may be interaction effects as well. Some reforms give new responsibilities to government agencies, while others give new regulatory responsibilities to make the private market work in a more desirable way.

Initial Legislation

It would probably be easier for politicians to increase payroll taxes if the new revenue were directed into individual accounts rather than into a collective trust fund. Thus individual accounts are seen as having a political advantage by some who favor increasing payroll taxes in order to have a better-financed Social Security system and more national savings. Similarly, some analysts want to use current and projected budget surpluses to finance individual accounts in order to block alternative uses of these surpluses. While the surpluses could be added to the Trust Fund, there may be more political interest in placing them in individual accounts. As discussed in section 1.2, initial legislation may also affect legislation of the rest of the government budget at the same time.

Future Legislation about Advance Funding

One concern about introducing legislation increasing advanced funding is that it might be offset by future Social Security legislation that would prevent the advanced funding from being maintained into the future.

A further issue is the extent to which the additional funds accumulated in Social Security would remain as part of increased national capital, which depends in part on the extent to which surpluses in Social Security would lead to decreases in other government taxation and in increases in other government spending. As described under Question 1, impacts of current Social Security legislation on future non-Social Security budgets are difficult to assess.

We begin by examining future legislation with a central Trust Fund buildup.

With a central fund, a critical concern is that advance funding (with a higher funding target) might not result in preservation of the higher target. The Panel thinks that there is a significant chance that some future Congress would use at least some of the funds to increase benefits or reduce taxes or possibly spend them for other purposes, diluting the effect on national capital.

It may be possible to reduce the chance that future Congresses would spend a large accumulated Trust Fund. Proclamation of a congressional intent to have a permanently larger trust fund may have some effect on future legislation. Second,

Congress could create a Social Security investment board charged with identifying legislation that harms Social Security's financial position. Third, the Office of the Actuary, which currently reports on actuarial balance, could change its reporting to include new targets for the Trust Fund accumulation. However, these institutions may be insufficient to adequately protect the Trust Fund from future spending.[46,47]

Advance funding through individual accounts is probably less likely to be spent by legislation directly increasing benefits or financing other spending than advance funding through a Trust Fund buildup. Concern about this issue is one of the main reasons some analysts support the creation of individual accounts.

Access to Funds before Retirement

With individual accounts, there would be pressure for access to the funds before retirement age, reducing national saving and retirement incomes. The Panel is concerned about the possibility of too much early access. With the accounts viewed as "the worker's own money," it is likely to be difficult for the political process to fully preserve the accounts just for retirement, disability and survivors. Indeed, with current voluntary 401(k) accounts, individuals can have early access for specified purposes and often can borrow against the funds, although such early access may be less likely in a nation-wide, mandated, individual account Social Security system. Early access limits the accumulation of funds for retirement purposes and the contribution to increased national savings.

With individual accounts, a critical concern is that the funds might not be preserved until retirement. The Panel thinks that some access to individual accounts before retirement age is likely to be allowed. The result would be less-adequate retirement incomes and less national savings than if the funds were preserved for retirement purposes.

Access to Funds at Retirement

With individual accounts, there would be pressure for access to the funds as a lump sum at retirement age. With the accounts viewed as "the worker's own money," it may well be difficult to require workers to annuitize their accounts and to require married workers to use joint and survivor annuities. There is no precedent in existing voluntary defined-contribution retirement savings plans in the United States for federal government mandates that the funds be annuitized. Mexico and Sweden have included mandatory annuitization in their national mandatory systems. Since these accounts are new, we do not yet know whether these restrictions will be maintained once benefits start to be paid. Without such requirements, retirees and their spouses would be at risk of outliving the individual account portion of their Social Security income. And, without some constraint on access to funds, there is a free rider problem that some people would spend their accounts rapidly and then become eligible for SSI benefits, thereby raising the cost of that program.

The contribution of Social Security reform to increased national savings is likely to be influenced by annuitization. With annuitization, the accumulated wealth in individual accounts is slowly distributed over the retirement lifetime of a worker or the worker and spouse. If there is access to lump sums, the contribution to national savings would depend on the rate at which people consumed from the lump sums, which might be lower or higher than with annuitization.

Legislation requiring that the funds accumulated in individual accounts be annuitized at or after retirement (and that these annuities be joint and survivor annuities) might be difficult to sustain politically as the public image of Social Security changed from that of a provider of monthly benefits to that of (partially) an organizer of individually owned accounts. This could leave retired workers, and in particular widowed spouses, exposed to substantial longevity risk.

Future Legislation in Response to Changing Economic and Demographic Factors

Any government-legislated system providing retirement income could be expected to need periodic legislation in response to changing economic and social conditions in order to serve their private and social purposes well. Since the current system's inception, Congress has changed tax rates many times, amended coverage rules, lowered the age of first eligibility for benefits, lowered as well as raised benefit formulas, and altered cost-of-living adjustments. Future changes in the form and structure of the Social Security system may help workers adapt to changing circumstances, but may also add uncertainty to workers and retirees regarding what might be legislated, making it difficult for households to make financial plans for retirement. Here we consider how the introduction of individual accounts might alter the pattern and frequency of legislation in the Social Security arena.

The frequency with which government-mandated retirement systems require legislative changes depends on the nature of their original design. The original Social Security system had no built-in mechanisms for dealing with either inflation or actuarial imbalances, so Congress periodically adjusted benefits and the wage base for inflation, and it occasionally adjusted tax rates to keep the system financially sound. In 1972, Congress created automatic mechanisms to adjust both benefits and the wage base for inflation. It has not created automatic mechanisms to adjust for changes in life expectancy or to deal with issues of long-run financial solvency.

A fully defined-contribution system will result in different political responses to changed circumstances than will a mixed system or a fully defined benefit system.

A fully defined contribution system would not have the same kinds of pressures to reconsider the program's basic elements. Once Congress set a contribution rate, money would begin flowing into individual accounts. If overall investment performance were better or worse than expected, then individuals would be better-off or worse-off at retirement. There would be no built-in pressure for Congress to revisit the contribution rate, as there is in a defined benefit system, because financial solvency would no longer be a governmental problem. Similarly, increasing life expectancy at retirement is converted into lower benefits. (This holds with annuity purchase and also with the level of spending that an individual could sustain if there were not annuitization.) Individuals could choose to work longer, save more, or retire on less, but they would not likely pressure government to force them to save more.

Although contribution rates might remain unchanged for a very long time, there might be more frequent pressures to change the benefit side of the system. Of course, government would no longer control the level of benefits directly, but it might reconsider and change the rules for early access, annuitization, and investment options from time to time. Thus, a fully defined- contribution system is likely to have less frequent legislation about contribution rates and directly about benefits. On the other hand, it is likely to have more frequent legislation that affects benefits by changing rules of access. In addition, factors that lead to low accumulations or retirement benefits (such as low market returns for certain individuals or cohorts) might generate calls to protect those near retirement in other ways, such as through general revenues.

In a mixed system having both defined-contribution and defined-benefit tiers, the frequency of legislation is more difficult to predict since it depends on how the two tiers relate to each other. If all of the advance funding is in the defined contribution portion, the defined-benefit portion is likely to need adjustment more frequently than if comparable advance funding were done in the defined-benefit portion as well. There may be pressures to increase the defined benefit portion when the defined-contribution portion has had low returns. On the other hand, there would be automatic adjustments by the market in the defined-contribution portion, while there might not be similar automatic adjustments in the defined-benefit portion. Thus, it is difficult to predict which system will require more frequent legislative adaptations.

Also, the difference in the way that individuals with different earnings levels are likely to be affected by future political changes differs across structures. If individual accounts were shielded from certain political interventions, then only the defined-benefit portion of Social Security might be adjusted in response to some shocks, such as low growth of the covered labor force; this risk might thus be allocated more to lower-income people than would be the case under a unified system. For example, a flat benefit, as was proposed by one of the groups on the 1994–96 Advisory Council on Social Security (the Personal Security Accounts plan) is likely to be changed differently from a progressive benefit. If a flat benefit is lowered in response to low payroll tax revenue, it seems likely to remain a flat benefit, while it seems unlikely to have equal dollar reductions in benefits with a progressive defined benefit system.

Without individual accounts, economic and demographic shocks often result in necessary legislative changes, because of fiscal pressures. For example, increasing life expectancy at retirement eventually causes a financial difficulty for the system, unless the system has been designed with automatic adjustments for life expectancy. Also, without individual accounts, increased advance funding and a higher funding target in the Trust Fund are likely to decrease the frequency of needed adjustments to Social Security. A higher target for the Trust Fund does not decrease the frequency of legislation needed to maintain the targeted funding. Holding constant the degree of automatic adjustment and other aspects of Social Security, however, legislation that results in larger projected funding will decrease the likelihood that the Trust Fund will be in danger of reaching zero funds. Therefore, with a higher target, it may be appropriate to have a larger band in allowed fluctuations of the Trust Fund without feeling the need for new legislation. Thus, increased advance funding of the Social Security Trust Fund can reduce the frequency of needed adjustments to Social Security.

In sum, the creation of individual accounts would change the political pressures affecting the response to market returns, wage growth, labor force growth, and life expectancy, and other factors.

Future Legislative Changes Due to Changes in the Political Climate

In addition to responding to future economic and demographic changes directly related to Social Security, future Congresses could change Social Security in response to changing political winds or severe non-Social Security fiscal problems. This adds a "political risk" to the current system: the risk that future Congresses will raise taxes or cut defined benefits of some or all individuals. This is particularly problematic if benefits for beneficiaries affects individuals late in their lives, when they have little time to adjust.

This risk could affect both high and low income households. High income households would suffer disproportionately if Congress chose to implement some sort of "means testing." Lower income households would suffer more if Congress chose to cut benefits across the board, because Social Security income is a greater fraction of their retirement resources. Shifting to a system of fully individual accounts may better protect individuals from this form of political risk. Changes in tax treatment of benefits remain a significant possibility with individual accounts. It is not clear whether a mixed system would better protect individuals than the current system.

Social Investing

As discussed in Question 2, the risk of social investing is that investments might have higher risks or lower expected returns than would be achieved if balancing risk and return were the only consideration. This risk is generally pointed to in the context of Trust Fund investment. Indeed, individuals are more likely to resist social investing pressures if the money is in their own accounts rather than in a pooled fund over which their sense of individual ownership is minimal. However, related risk would also be present with the introduction of individual accounts, even if organized by the private market.

First, there would be less political resistance to the provision of an option for individual accounts of an index fund reflecting social concerns than to the selection of such a fund by the Trust Fund. Second, individual workers might respond to social pressures to make social investments when doing so was not in their best interest. For example, there is concern about the extent to which workers currently invest heavily in shares of their employers, possibly in response to social pressures. Third, legislation might require social investing by firms holding individual accounts, as has been done with a requirement for local lending by banks under the Community Reinvestment Act. Overall, it is not clear whether individual accounts decrease the risk of investing that is not in the best interests of workers. However, such investing may be viewed as more problematic when the decision is made by the government than when it is made by individuals in their own accounts.

Corporate Governance

As discussed under Question 2, there are concerns that Trust Fund investment in stocks might be used to affect corporate decisions in adverse ways. There are similar concerns, but not identical, with government-organized individual accounts. Privately organized individual accounts do not generate such concerns.

3.7 Recapping

Taking into account all of the issues involved in setting up individual accounts, the Panel is divided as to whether individual accounts should be part of Social Security reform.

The Panel's split on whether to recommend individual accounts does not arise primarily from differences in economic analyses. Rather, it derives from the different weights placed on different values by the Panel members, as well as from different political predictions. We now gather together the key arguments that have led different Panel members to different conclusions.

Reasons for favoring individual accounts:

1. Individual accounts may be more likely to be financed with additional resources (and so add to national savings).

2. If advance funding were held in a central Trust Fund, it might not be sustained, but might be used for some other purpose, such as an increase in benefits or other spending, as in the past.

3. Stocks held in a central Trust Fund might be used to directly influence corporate decision-making based on concerns other than financial risk and return; and investment policy might be based on concerns other than financial risk and return.

4. Legislation without individual accounts might not restore the confidence of many, particularly younger, workers in the future of Social Security, affecting support for the program.

5. Individual accounts encourage individual responsibility and allow individual ownership and individual choice.

6. Individual accounts permit people with different degrees of risk aversion to hold different portfolios.

7. Individual accounts may discourage tax evasion and increase incentives to participate in the system.

8. Individual accounts may reduce the frequency of certain kinds of Social Security legislation and better insulate some individuals from the risk of future legislated benefit cuts.

Reasons for and against specifically government-organized individual accounts:

1. Government-organized accounts would cost less to administer than privately organized accounts and would give workers fewer investment options.

2. Stocks held in government-organized individual accounts might be used to directly influence corporate decision-making based on concerns other than financial risk and return; and investment policy might be based on concerns other than financial risk and return.

3. By providing less in services than is common with many 401(k) plans, government-organized accounts might lead some people to view the government as inefficient in its provision of retirement income, because they were not fully aware of the lower per capita costs.

Reasons for opposing individual accounts:

1. Individual accounts would increase administrative costs, increase the exposure of workers to market risks, and expose workers to the risk of poor investment choices.

2. Early access to individual accounts and the receipt of benefits as a lump-sum might not preserve adequate benefits for workers and for surviving spouses. This would also decrease the contribution to national savings.

3. The creation and possible later growth of individual accounts might be financed, in part, by lowering benefits in the disability and/or young survivors insurance programs.

4. The creation and possible later growth of individual accounts might result in an erosion of the benefit levels provided to those with low earnings.

5. Individual accounts would undercut the sense of community responsibility and shared concerns embodied in Social Security; large variation in benefits between members of different cohorts employing the same investment strategy is undesirable.

6. Individual accounts might be financed by a diversion of resources that would otherwise go to the Trust Fund, so that they would not contribute to increased national savings.

7. Restoring actuarial balance in the existing system might restore workers' confidence in the future of Social Security; by diverting revenues and introducing new risks, individual accounts might not improve confidence either in the remaining defined benefit portion of Social Security or in the overall system.

8. By possibly diverting resources from the Trust Fund to individual accounts, the defined benefits will be less well financed and more likely to have financial difficulty requiring legislation.

Panel members weighing these values, political predictions, and economic implications differently have reached different conclusions as to the desirability of individual accounts. Some of these considerations weigh more or less heavily depending on details of a proposal, especially the source of funding.

Question 4   Issues of Choice

If individual accounts are adopted, how much choice should workers be allowed in selecting investments, and in the timing and form of payments from the accounts? Should individual accounts be voluntary or mandatory?

4.1 Choice in Investment Options

While one could have a defined-contribution system with no individual choice of investment portfolio, allowing some individual choice would enable workers with different degrees of risk aversion to hold portfolios with different risks. In addition, workers could alter their portfolios as they aged, had wealth changes, and/or desired a different degree of risk. This advantage of individual choice would come with the disadvantages of higher administrative costs and the possibility that some people would make poor choices, particularly those with little or no experience in investing. Both disadvantages could be somewhat mitigated, however, by limiting the choices of portfolios for individual accounts.

The Panel is concerned that many investors may fail to understand the risk characteristics of investments.

Recognizing the advantages of portfolio diversification and the various political issues involved, index funds with broad indexes are good bases for portfolio choice in government-organized individual accounts. Having individual accounts organized privately would decrease some of the political concerns that might lead to limiting investment choice in government-organized accounts to index funds. Widely diversified managed portfolios then would represent another possible choice, although it should be recognized that managed funds have higher administrative and brokerage costs than do index funds, and that on average, managed funds have historically not done better than index funds. Moreover, it is to be expected that many workers will not adequately appreciate the importance of diversification in selecting a suitable tradeoff between risk and return. One possible response to this concern is to restrict investment in stocks to widely diversified portfolios, leaving to a regulatory body the definition of the degree of diversification that is adequate to protect workers in their investment choices.

Other investment options offered in the market, such as stable value funds and certificates of deposit, have fixed rates of return. Inflation-indexed fixed-interest options are also available. Insofar as the financial institutions are sufficiently well capitalized so that the probability of significant failure to meet payment promises is very low, these options are an alternative approach to wide diversification.

Restrictions on privately organized investment choices made available to workers will involve new regulatory oversight of financial institutions. In addition, there will be calls for the government to insure promised returns for mandated savings that are invested in guaranteed products, particularly after a financial disappointment. Guarantees arranged in advance, including a premium charged for the guarantee are preferable to bailouts after the fact.

Bailouts, or the expectations of bailouts could lead to mispricing of products and excessive risk. Additional federal regulation would be a change especially in the insurance industry, where regulation is performed primarily by the states, not the federal government.

The Panel thinks that if there are individual accounts organized by the government, individuals should have choices that include government bonds (including inflation-protected bonds) and separate index funds containing private bonds, stocks in the United States, and possibly investments abroad.[48]

The Panel thinks that if there are individual accounts organized by private firms, the choices should be restricted to widely diversified mutual funds and guaranteed products, such as federal government bonds (including inflation-protected bonds), stable value funds and certificates of deposit (CDs).[49]

Even with a limited range of alternatives, there will be a need for worker education. The poor choice of portfolios by many workers, in the form of heavy investment in the shares of their employers or conservatism that seems excessive, suggests the importance of such education. The need for worker education raises two issues. The first is who will have the job of providing the education—the government, employers, or financial institutions. The second is that the cost of providing education of a sufficient magnitude to significantly affect workers' behavior would be large relative to the size of individual accounts in a plan financed by a small percentage of workers' earnings. However, this education would help workers make better financial choices outside of Social Security as well.

4.2 Choice of Annuitization

In the earlier discussion of a low-cost system, it was assumed that there would be mandatory annuitization according to rules set by legislation.

Two classes of issues arise when considering individual choice about the provision of retirement income: (1) the choices individuals make for themselves and (2) the protection of spouses in the event of the death of a worker.

Left to their own devices, people do not take much advantage of private annuities, exposing themselves to the risk of outliving their assets. The current provision of monthly Social Security benefits reduces the importance of this risk. We do not have sufficient historical evidence to know whether people would voluntarily annuitize their individual accounts sufficiently to roughly maintain the annuitization level provided by Social Security monthly benefits.

The current market for individual annuities which are paid as annuities is extremely small (Mitchell et al., forthcoming).[50] Adverse selection and the presence of Social Security benefits are part of the explanation, but the market is smaller than can be explained by these factors alone.

Proposals take three different forms with regard to allowing choice about retirement income. Some proposals allow some lump-sum withdrawals, leaving the worker free to choose the extent of annuitization of that portion, whatever rules apply to the remaining balances. An intermediate position is to give workers a choice between annuitization and periodic withdrawal (monthly, for example), with a limit on the size of the allowed withdrawal to limit the risk of outliving the retirement wealth. Other proposals mandate annuitization of the entire accumulation.

An advantage of allowing individual choice with regard to annuitization is that individuals can have access to a lump sum to spend as they wish. Disadvantages of voluntary annuitization are that such choice introduces adverse selection into the pricing of annuities and puts at risk the long-lived who do not annuitize. Since the long-lived are overwhelmingly widows, and since, as noted earlier, the poverty rate among widows is already very high, this is an issue not just of individual choice, but also of allocation within the family. Moreover, any lack of annuitization is likely to increase the cost of the SSI program. The low level of voluntary annuitization in the United States today suggests that many people do not understand the insurance advantages of annuitization, although in part it reflects the existing annuitization by Social Security. Just as mandated savings are needed to ensure adequate retirement savings, some degree of mandated annuitization or restriction on the rate of withdrawal is needed to ensure adequate savings when workers reach advanced ages.

The Panel thinks retirees should not be able to take all of their retirement benefits as a lump sum. Annuitization (through either a defined-benefit system or mandated annuitization of at least part of accumulations) or restrictions on the rate of monthly withdrawal should be part of the system.

An important issue with mandated annuitization of individual accounts is the political stability of such a proposal as the public's view of Social Security shifts. For example, would an individual with limited life expectancy or extraordinary immediate needs be forced to annuitize?

Evidence from the United Kingdom suggests that people purchasing annuities do not purchase inflation protection when they have the opportunity.

Even though real government bonds and real annuities have been offered for some time in the United Kingdom, individuals overwhelmingly choose nominal annuities. Yet the importance of the indexing of benefits is steadily increasing as life expectancy at retirement continues to rise. Even with a 2 percent inflation rate, the real value of a nominal annuity will decline by 18 percent in 10 years, 33 percent in 20 years, and 45 percent in 30 years (when someone retiring at 62 would be 92). Indeed, with wives typically being younger than their husbands, the time from a husband's annuitization decision to a wife's death will be more than 30 years for a considerable number of women. With 4 percent inflation, these declines in real value become 34, 56, and 71 percent after 10, 20, and 30 years, respectively.

While a predictable rate of inflation can be handled by a given annual rate of increase in nominal benefits, the unpredictability of inflation makes indexing to inflation of greater value.

Some people may want a change in the real purchasing power of their annuity as they age. Such a decision should be explicit, not a byproduct of whatever level of inflation may have occurred.

One needs to be concerned about the ability of the government or the private market to keep the promises made by indexed annuities. In contrast with a defined-benefit system, in which benefits can be adjusted to some extent for poor portfolio experience, annuitization of a defined-contribution account is meant to be a guaranteed income source. The ability to guarantee future benefits depends in part on the nature of assets being held to help finance such a guarantee. The presence of indexed Treasury bonds makes it clear that indexed annuities can be provided by both Social Security and the private market, provided the Treasury will ensure an adequate supply of these bonds.

The Panel thinks that mandated annuities should be real annuities, that is, annuities indexed for inflation.

Given the choice, many workers tend to select single-life as opposed to joint-and-survivor annuities that continue payment to a worker's spouse after the worker's death.

Single-life annuities were very popular in employer-provided retirement plans prior to the passage of the Employee Retirement Income Security Act (ERISA) in 1974. The portion of retirees who took joint-and-survivor annuities in private pension plans grew after ERISA made these annuities the default option, and grew further after the 1983 Retirement Equity Act, which required notarized spousal consent in order to decline a joint-and-survivor annuity.

The degree to which workers choose joint-and-survivor annuitization is very sensitive to the way choices are presented to them.

The importance of the effects of annuitization choices can be seen in the New Beneficiary Data System. A sample of new Social Security beneficiaries was interviewed in 1982 and reinterviewed in 1991. While the median value of real pension income had fallen 23 percent for intact couples between the interview dates, the median value of real pension income had fallen by 75 percent in those cases in which the wife had been widowed between the interview dates (Coile and Diamond, 1998).

In short, when evaluating a shift from today's defined-benefit system to a defined-contribution approach, it is important to consider not only the effects on the worker, but also those on the worker's family. In the mixed defined-benefit/defined-contribution proposals of the Individual Account and Personal Security Account plans, the family structures of the defined-benefit portions are similar to current law, but the defined-contribution portions are different. Although there has been considerable discussion of changing the treatment of the family within Social Security, such changes seem much more likely should there be a shift to individual accounts.

To the extent that large lump-sum withdrawals are allowed, there is concern for the protection of a surviving lower-earning spouse. Protection of spouses in an individual account system can be accomplished in a number of different ways, including dividing the accounts between husband and wife and limiting the spending of funds from the accounts. One form of protection is for the accounts to be inherited by a spouse (if there is one) on the death of a worker. This rule would apply for death before retirement and as a protection for accounts that have limited withdrawal rates. Also, restrictions on the rate of withdrawal from accounts can reflect the need to protect a survivor. If there is mandatory annuitization, lower-earning spouses can be protected by requiring some degree of joint-and-survivor annuitization. Before any movement toward individual choice, its effect on the economic position of widows needs to be assessed very carefully.

The Panel reiterates that protection of a lower-earning spouse is important, and if a system does not mandate considerable benefits for a surviving spouse, at least it should have a division of accounts between spouses in some form.

4.3 Voluntary Individual Accounts

Through IRAs and 401(k)s, the United States has a system of tax-favored voluntary defined-contribution retirement accounts. Such accounts might be expanded or altered at the same time as Social Security reform. One possibility is that the Social Security Administration offer an IRA option which includes access to the same investment opportunities as are offered through TSP. Such an expansion of voluntary savings opportunities might, but need not, be associated with a decrease in mandated retirement savings. The Panel has not addressed such accounts, nor the use of general revenues to partially finance accounts that might be voluntary.

In contrast with simply adding to the available tax-favored retirement savings options, some Social Security reform proposals substitute a voluntary option for some of the existing Social Security defined-benefit system. Such proposals would allow people to choose to divert a portion of their payroll tax into individual accounts while simultaneously giving up a portion of their Social Security defined-benefits, sometimes referred to as a voluntary carve-out. Such carve-out proposals face the implementation issues of mandatory accounts and raise new questions. One is how to design the way opting out affects Social Security benefits. If a worker chooses to direct an allowed portion of Social Security payroll taxes to an individual account, defined-benefits must be reduced as compared to those who did not choose an individual account. Second is potential administrative difficulty and costs of introducing an additional option. Allowing voluntary opting out raises administrative costs. Many of the administrative costs are setup costs for having individual accounts, so that this part of the costs are similar whether there is voluntary or mandatory individual accounts. Similarly, if the option is privately organized accounts, a similar regulatory and enforcement structure is needed for voluntary as for mandatory accounts. Third is the possible political pressure for guarantees and protections for those electing accounts, possibly mistakenly, and more generally the effect of voluntary opt-out on the politics of Social Security as social insurance. Significant public education would be needed to help workers with the decision on whether to opt out.

Allowing voluntary diversion of payroll tax contributions from the defined benefit program to individual accounts would involve considerably more administrative cost per account than would mandatory accounts.

In terms of implementation, regulation and enforcement, voluntary accounts have all the cost and design issues of mandatory accounts, plus some additional costs as a consequence of a need to receive, process, monitor and correct reports of whether an individual has chosen to use an individual account. Moreover, some economies of scale are lost as a result of less than full selection of accounts.

In considering the terms on which opting out is available, one needs to consider the financial impact on Social Security. First, as described above, part of Social Security contributions are a tax to pay for unfunded obligations. An adjustment would need to be made so that those opting out continued to pay their share of these costs. Second, it is important to recognize the adverse selection risk. That is, those standing to gain more financially would be more likely to opt out. Who stands to gain more depends on the determination of Social Security defined benefits that are lost and the rules affecting administration for those who opt out.

Allowing voluntary diversion of payroll taxes to individual accounts would have a serious adverse selection risk. Unless the rules governing the decrease in defined benefits for those who opt out correctly adjust for this risk, the voluntary opt out might worsen the financial position of the defined benefit portion of Social Security. Similarly, voluntary opt-out and risky investment choices by those possibly eligible for Supplemental Security Income (SSI) benefits might increase the cost of the SSI program. In any case, benefit rules to account for selection risk would be either very complex or very approximate.

Judging by the experience in Britain, voluntary accounts have the potential for serious political and legal ramifications. Depending on how defined-benefits are reduced for those opting out, some individuals may end up worse off than if they did not opt out. Indeed concern about this issue has led some proposals to include a "guarantee" to protect those who opt out, a guarantee that needs to be priced as part of such a proposal. Without a guarantee, there would still be political pressure to offset losses if market losses were widespread. Since individuals will be making a somewhat difficult decision, there would be a need for some form of education for individuals considering such opt-outs. Some information would need to come from the government. If individuals were opting out to accounts organized by private institutions, then those institutions would also have an interest in advising workers to select them over alternative financial institutions and over not opting out. Individuals who made a poor choice, either ex ante or ex

post, may institute a class-action lawsuit relating to the
nature of the advice they received. Indeed in Britain, the
experience with opt-outs from the defined-benefit (SERPS)
system into individual accounts has been called the "mis-
selling scandal" and has resulted in compensation. British
experience is likely to be a cautionary lesson for American
institutions, but some risk remains.

**The Panel does not recommend allowing voluntary diver-
sion of payroll tax contributions from the defined benefit
program to individual accounts.**[51]

If there is voluntary diversion of payroll tax contributions to
individual accounts, the decrease in defined benefits for
those opting out needs to account properly for adverse selection and increased costs.

Question 5

Private vs. Government Collection, Management, and Distribution

If individual accounts are adopted, should the reformed system move toward private and decentralized collection of contributions, management of investments, and payment of annuities, or should these functions be administered by a government agency (the Treasury or the Social Security Administration)?

In section 3.2, a low-cost/low-services system of individual accounts is described in which the federal government collects the deposits to individual accounts, holds the accounts in a set of allowable funds, converts the accumulation into annuities, and pays the annuities to beneficiaries. Each of the steps in this process could be privatized. This section contrasts centralized and market performance of these steps; the discussion also addresses the need for oversight and regulation should a step be performed privately.

5.1 Collection

If the accounts were organized by the government, there would be no point in having private collection of deposits. If the accounts were organized by private financial institutions, the deposits could be collected by the federal government and handed over to those financial institutions (possibly less a fee for the costs of collection and transmittal). Alternatively, the funds could go directly from employers or employees to private financial institutions. If the government collected and transmitted the funds once a year, paralleling the low-cost/low-services system described earlier, the additional costs associated with transmittal itself are not likely to be large. In addition, there would be costs of confirming the accurate receipt of deposits (amount, identification of worker, and choice of financial institution) and dealing with questions and errors in the process. Without any comparable experience, it is difficult to predict the cost of such a distribution system, but it is likely to be significant.

In contrast to government collection, we can consider direct payment by employers to private financial institutions.

A plan requiring employers to be accountable for directly depositing workers' contributions into individual accounts might not be a large burden for some large firms with stable workforcees and electronic bookkeeping, many of which already have 401(k) plans and perform direct deposit of wage payments into worker bank accounts. However, this procedure would represent a significant burden for some small employers.

Even with large firms, a significant fraction of workers are not paid with direct deposit. Moreover, the number of financial institutions holding individual accounts for the workers of a single firm is likely to be larger than the number of banks at which they receive direct deposit. Similarly, firms deal with only a small number of providers (often just one) when making 401(k) deposits. It may be noted that 401(k) plans are offered to only 7 percent of people working for firms with fewer than 25 employees, but to 53 percent of people working for firms with at least 250 employees (EBRI, 1994).

In addition, with direct deposits from employers, financial institutions would have to reconcile reports from many employers, rather than dealing with a single report from the federal government. Among the complications this entails are dealing with workers with multiple employers during the year whose total earnings exceed the maximum taxable earnings base. In large part, reconciliation of employer reports would duplicate that already performed by the Social Security Administration. With direct deposits by employers, the cost of reconciliation by financial institutions would add significantly to the charges for individual accounts.

Another issue is whether individuals would be restricted to a single financial institution or could have multiple accounts with multiple financial institutions, an additional diversification that some analysts consider useful. If workers were charged the fixed-cost component of their accounts, workers with multiple accounts would be paying more in charges. Yet some workers would not be sufficiently aware of this issue to consolidate their accounts. This situation would be especially likely to occur with workers who switched employers frequently. Thus there would be cost savings from limiting workers to a single financial institution. On the other hand, if small accounts were subsidized, for example by requiring that all charges be proportional to the size of the account, then multiple accounts would increase the costs for everyone. Without having the funds flow through a single source, presumably the federal government, there is no simple mechanism that can identify workers with multiple accounts; rather, it would be necessary for the federal government to duplicate some of the collection information gathered by financial institutions.

Beyond the costs that would fall on employers, there is the question of who would perform the verification, oversight, and enforcement functions now performed by the Social Security Administration and the Internal Revenue Service (IRS). The need to confirm that employers had transmitted the appropriate amounts to the correct financial institution and that the institution had recorded deposits and investment returns correctly would fall on workers unless some agency were providing oversight. Similarly, workers would bear the risk from failure of firms to transmit withheld funds into individual accounts. Moreover, the IRS would now have an additional tax evasion realm to monitor, which would require additional resources. Since millions of workers do not file income tax returns, linkage to the income tax is not a simple solution by itself.

With direct deposits by employers, there would also be substantial regulatory and enforcement costs for the government to assure that the accounts are established and maintained and funds are deposited in a timely manner.

The Panel thinks the direct economic gains from mandatory direct deposits by employers would not be worth the increase in cost, at least until and if widespread adoption of technology led to a substantial decrease in costs.

In addition to a uniform system in which all employers would send withheld funds to the Treasury or to private institutions holding individual accounts, one could have a system in which some employers would send withheld funds to the Treasury, while others would send them directly to private institutions. The issues with such a system are not reviewed here.

5.2 Organization of Accounts

There would be both advantages and disadvantages to shifting individual portfolio choice from a set of alternatives provided by the government to choices available in the private market, subject to federal regulation of available investments.

Among the advantages would be the opportunity to invest in managed (as opposed to indexed) accounts and possibly even individually designed portfolios; the opportunity for rapid adoption of technological innovations that might occur in the availability of indexing; and wider choice for individuals, with the federal government having a lesser role in selecting alternatives and holding portfolios. It must be recognized, however, that some people would not designate a private financial institution, so there would have to be a default option of either a government-organized portfolio or allocation of those not designating a private provider to private plans. Since people with small accounts might choose a government-provided default for cost reasons, such accounts would have to be in a well-designed portfolio, possibly integrated with the TSP.

Among the disadvantages of a shift to private organization of accounts would be the higher costs and the greater risk of poor investment choices by some individuals, as well as possibilities for fraud and misrepresentation. In addition to these economic effects, the holding of the accounts outside the government could influence the politics of preserving the funds for retirement purposes and the mandating of annuitization. With mandated investments organized by financial institutions, there would be considerable pressure for additional regulation of those institutions. The extent of the pressure for additional regulation would likely depend on the range of investment choices that were allowed. As discussed in section 3.6, it is not clear whether concerns about social investing would be larger or smaller, although the nature of the concerns would be different.

As with private collection of funds, a major issue in considering private organization of accounts is how high the associated costs would be and how those costs would be allocated among individuals with different levels of contributions and accumulations. The Advisory Council on Social Security assumes that the 5 percent Personal Savings Accounts financed by 5 percent of payroll and organized by private financial institutions would involve an annual charge of 1 percent of assets under management, with the same percentage for all accounts.

The Panel thinks the charges for privately organized individual accounts would be larger, in percentage terms, for smaller than for larger accounts unless the government required uniform percentage charges.

To see how regulation might work, it is useful to note how the market currently offers better opportunities to those with larger investment balances.

Currently, banks, insurance companies, and mutual funds often require minimum account balances and offer better opportunities for larger accounts than smaller ones. Thus, the primary impact of regulation requiring uniform percentage charges would be the requirement that financial institutions accept all accounts on the same terms.

If there are individual accounts organized by private financial institutions, the Panel recommends regulations that would require any financial institution accepting such accounts (1) to apply the same charges (per dollar of

deposits and per dollar of account balances) for all workers, and (2) to accept all workers who wished to use the institution, regardless of the size of their accounts.

An alternative approach to improving the net market return for small accounts is to provide a governmental "match" for low earners. Such a match would need to determine rules relating the size of the match to the size of the account and the size of the deposit, and, possibly, the choice of portfolio and financial institution. In addition, a source of revenue would be needed to finance the match. With this alternative approach, an explicit subsidy would replace the implicit cross-subsidy from a requirement of uniform charges. A dissenting view holds that this alternative approach would be preferable because the recommended uniformity of percentage changes hides the distortion of the relative price of financial services. There are questions about the political sustainability of a subsidizing match. That is, the "framing" of this issue as providing the "same" opportunities to all workers might result in a different political outcome from the framing of this issue as subsidizing the market outcome. One approach makes outcomes more transparent, while the other makes redistribution more transparent.

If the recommendation of uniform charges were to be implemented without any cap on the level of charges, the Panel does not think there would be serious risk of inadequate supply of financial institutions willing to handle these accounts. However, if this recommendation were to be implemented along with a cap on the level of charges, then there might be a supply problem in that many financial institutions might choose not to offer these services because of a risk that the business would not be profitable if the firm were to end up with a large fraction of accounts which had high costs relative to their charges.

The Panel thinks that the estimate of the Advisory Council on Social Security—of an annual charge of 1 percent of the account balance, for Personal Security Accounts funded by 5 percent of the payroll tax—is roughly correct on average once the system is mature. This figure is similar to fees paid on average with private investments today. With smaller accounts (2 or 3 percent of payroll), charges would be higher in percentage terms since much of the cost would be fixed per account.

Certain types of portfolios organized by some firms would charge less than 1 percent, and others would charge more. In particular, on average index funds have lower fees than managed funds holding the same class of assets. One cannot gauge the average costs by considering only the best opportunities currently in the market or only the worst ones.

A 1 percent per year fee for funds under management corresponds to roughly a 20 percent decrease in the accumulation in an account at the end of a 40-year career, as compared with an account without charges. The administrative costs are not the sole basis for evaluating individual accounts, as is discussed elsewhere.

With a 40-year career, deposits into individual accounts would be subjected to a 1 percent fee roughly 20 times, on average. While this amount is sizable, we reiterate that it is roughly the average fee charged in the market today. Table 2 shows the loss in final value for different levels of annual management fees and front loads. We note that this estimate of 1 percent of account balances for 5 percent individual accounts is considerably larger than the estimate of costs for government-organized accounts, as discussed in section 3.2

Table 2
Decline in Value of Accounts Due to Fees After a 40-Year Work Career[a]

Type and level of fees	Percentage decline in account value due to fees
Front-load fees (percent of new contributions) of:	
1 percent	1
10 percent	10
20 percent	20
Annual management fees (percent of account balance) of:	
0.1 percent	2.2
0.5 percent	10.5
1.0 percent	19.6

a. Assuming real wage growth of 2.1 percent and a real annual return on investments of 4 percent. With a larger difference between the rate of return and the wage growth rate, the charge ratio with annual management fees is slightly larger, and conversely.

above and does not include the cost of transmitting funds to the accounts.

On a lifetime basis, with accounts financed by 5 percent of payroll, a 1 percent of account balance annual charge is roughly equivalent to an annual front load charge that starts at $230 for the average covered worker, and grows with average wages. In contrast, a rough order of magnitude for the cost of government-organized individual accounts with limited services would be in the range of $25–50 per worker per year, also growing with average wages. The low cost/low services plan described above would provide considerably fewer services than a privately organized system. Costs would be higher for the government-organized system with the provision of more services.

With accounts financed by 5 percent of payroll, an annual charge of $25–50 (that grew at the same rate as wages) would be equivalent to a front load of roughly 3.5 percent and would lower the value of accounts by this amount, considerably less than the roughly 20 percent reduction from a 1 percent of assets annual fee.

The relative importance of the cost difference between government and private handling of individual accounts would be greater the smaller the percentage of payroll that was allocated to individual accounts.

With the startup of an individual account system, accounts would be small at the beginning and growing thereafter. Thus, charges that were proportional to account balances, a constant percentage over time and covered the costs of the accounts over the lifetime of a worker would not cover costs in the early years. Therefore, we would expect that some firms would make use of front-load charges, particularly during the startup of such a system, or that charges on balances would be higher in the early years, declining thereafter.

In light of the importance of administrative costs, some analysts have proposed a cap on allowable charges.

While the government could limit charges on individual accounts, such regulation would be complex. For example, different types of mutual funds have different cost structures and would need different caps (stocks vs. bonds, index vs. non-index, domestic vs. foreign investments.) In addition, some investment vehicles, such as stable value funds and certificates of deposit (CDs), do not have separate explicit charges, but incorporate administrative costs by lowering the interest rate offered. Moreover, with any limit on charges, there is the possibility that many firms might not offer to handle these accounts, limiting the choices available in the market.

Having privately organized accounts would require the government to create the regulatory and enforcement mechanisms for the privately organized accounts, protecting workers, but adding to government costs. Such regulation may include further rules on uniform disclosure of fees to help workers make comparisons.

Given the above advantages and disadvantages to the private market handling of individual accounts and the limited ability to estimate total costs, the Panel does not take a stand on whether individual accounts would best be organized by the government or private firms. The Panel recognizes that the initial implementation of a privately organized individual account system would be more expensive and difficult than initial implementation of a government-organized account system. Thus there would be some advantages in limiting the immediate creation of new institutions by beginning with government-organized accounts, which could eventually be shifted to the private market, although such a shift would involve some duplication of effort.

Recognizing all of the issues involved, including the difficulty of initial implementation, the Panel thinks that if individual accounts are created, they should start as government-organized accounts. Within a few years of full implementation, there should be serious consideration of a shift to privately organized accounts.[52]

In addition to an option of whether to have an individual account, some proposals include an option to choose a privately organized account rather than a government-organized account. Privately organized accounts may appeal to some workers because they value a higher level of services and are willing to pay for them in the form of higher administrative costs. Other workers may not fully appreciate the costs and benefits of such a choice. In addition there is a problem of "adverse selection." With charges proportional to account balances and costs that include a large fixed component, large accounts are cross-subsidizing the costs of small accounts. If the private market attracts large accounts, it is removing this cross-subsidy. To deal with this problem of "cream skimming," either there could be charges for accounts that opt-out of the government system or some source of revenue could be used to subsidize small accounts, in order to retain the cross-subsidy to low earners.

5.3 Annuitization

Annuitization of individual accounts might be accomplished in three different ways. First, the federal government could decide what benefits to pay for given accumulations, with Social Security bearing the risk inherent in projecting mortality and selecting a portfolio. Second, the federal government could contract with private providers to receive accounts from the government in return for paying the annuities. These annuities would be priced on a group basis. These payments could go directly to beneficiaries or to the government for transmittal to beneficiaries; in the latter case, the government would provide the payments directly to beneficiaries along with defined benefits. The private providers would bear the mortality and return risks, although there would be residual risk that a private insurance company would be unable to meet its obligations for annuity payments. It would be undesirable to put that residual risk on individuals, particularly those late in life. Therefore, the government should absorb that residual risk. Currently, insurance companies receive oversight from state governments, not the federal government; with such a residual risk for the federal government, there would be a call for federal oversight instead of or in addition to state oversight. Third, individuals could be left free to contract with insurance companies on their own, purchasing annuities from their accounts. This approach would employ individual rather than group purchase of annuities. In insurance markets generally, group products are considerably less expensive than individual products. This outcome reflects both lower costs for insurance companies in dealing with groups and greater competition for large group accounts than for smaller individual accounts.

Administrative costs of privately supplied individual annuities (ignoring issues of adverse selection) are estimated to be 5 to 10 percent of the purchase price currently, varying with the nature of the portfolio used for comparison purposes (Mitchell, Poterba, Warshawsky, and Brown, forthcoming). The Panel thinks this is a ballpark figure for what individual mandated annuities would cost. Currently, adverse selection results in mortality experience for annuity purchasers that adds roughly 10 percent to the price of annuities as compared with population mortality experience. It is difficult to know whether the market for annuities would expand significantly (decreasing adverse selection) without a mandate.

Like many insurance products, annuities are offered far more cheaply on a group basis than on an individual basis. An issue with a large national program is how to organize for group provision of annuities if it is decided to have annuities provided by the private market, not the government. One issue is the sheer size of the program, calling for the use of multiple groups and multiple providers, rather than a single provider of annuities for all retirees. If multiple groups are used, then, to preserve as much of the advantage of groups purchase as possible, the government needs to allocate people to different groups, rather than allowing the market to form the groups (Diamond, 1992). Since there is little reason for a geographic concentration of benefit recipients, people could be allocated to different groups randomly, giving everyone roughly the same opportunities.

In light of the cost issue, the Panel thinks that if annuitization is mandated and if it is provided by private firms, the annuities should be supplied as group annuities to the extent possible. This could be done by market bidding for groups with government-organized individual accounts. With privately organized accounts, the government could encourage or mandate the formation of groups.

Conclusion

There is no single reform plan that is recommended by the Panel. Indeed, the Panel is divided as to whether individual accounts should be recommended at all. Nevertheless, the Panel agrees that it is important to avoid large, abrupt changes in tax rates and benefit levels if Social Security is to fulfill its purpose as a secure foundation for retirement income, together with private pensions and individual savings. The sooner legislation takes effect, the smaller the tax rate changes and/or benefit cuts that would restore actuarial balance. The current Social Security tax rate is 12.4 percent, 6.2 percent each for employers and employees, each. If the tax rate were increased by 2.2 percentage points to 14.6 percent, acuarial balance would be restored over the 75-year time horizon. In contrast, if there is no legislation until 2030, the pay-as-you-go tax rate needed then would be about 17 percent and would rise to nearly 19 percent by 2075. Thus it is important to enact remedies soon.

Prompt legislative action will permit more gradual tax and/or benefit changes and allow more advance notice of benefit changes. The longer the delay in legislation, the more difficult the economic and political problems of reform will become.

The Panel urges that legislation restoring actuarial balance and containing whatever reforms are agreed upon be passed as soon as possible.

This report contains analyses of many issues, although it is by no means exhaustive of the questions that need to be answered in the design of legislation. Inevitably, the issues not taken up reflect the dynamics of Panel discussion rather than a logical omission of the least important issues. The logic of our analyses can be seen in the following highlights of our analyses and conclusions. We reiterate that Panel recommendations are not necessarily unanimous, but have the support of at least three-fourths of the members of the Panel. Some alternative views were presented above.

Increased advance funding would permit lower taxes and/or higher benefits in the future than without increased advance funding and can increase national saving. A major increase in advance funding, however, requires increased taxes or decreased benefits, or an additional source of revenue in the near term. If the federal budget does not largely offset the impact on national savings, the Panel recommends increased advance funding of Social Security.

Increased advance funding can happen within the Trust Fund or in individual accounts. Some Panel members prefer it to happen within the Trust Fund while some others prefer it to happen within individual accounts. Another view prefers continuation of pay-as-you-go.

The Panel has considered a number of issues related to diversifying investment portfolios. With Trust Fund investment in stocks and corporate bonds or government-organized individual accounts, careful design of the governance institution for diversified investment is extremely important. If the Trust Fund invests in stocks and corporate bonds, the

Panel recommends use of a governance structure similar to that of the Thrift Savings Plan (TSP). If individual accounts are organized by the government, the Panel also recommends a governance structure similar to that of the TSP. If individual accounts are organized by private firms, the Panel thinks that regulatory oversight is extremely important and that the choices should be restricted to widely diversified mutual funds and guaranteed products and that regulations require any financial institution accepting such accounts (1) to apply the same charges (per dollar of deposits and per dollar of account balances) for all workers, and (2) to accept all workers who wished to use the institution, regardless of the size of their accounts.

Taking the above into account, the Panel recommends use of diversified investment portfolios, including stocks and corporate bonds. Again, some members prefer that this be done through Trust Fund investment, while other prefer that it be done by allowing individuals to hold stocks and corporate bonds in individual accounts. If individual accounts are adopted, the Panel recommends allowing individuals to invest at least part of the funds in stocks and corporate bonds. If a central Trust Fund is built up, the Panel recommends investing part of it in stocks and corporate bonds, subject to a cap of 5 to 10 percent in the holding of any single stock, although a dissenting view disagrees because of concerns over the economic consequences of the ensuing political decisions.

The Panel does not favor allowing voluntary diversion of payroll tax contributions to individual accounts.

Much of the discussion of individual accounts has focused on the accumulation phase, without paying a similar amount of attention to the payment of benefits. Introduction of individual accounts needs to be carefully integrated with both disability benefits and benefits for children after the death of a parent—any reductions in those benefits should be an explicit decision, not a byproduct of changes in retirement benefits. Introduction of individual accounts must consider carefully the rules governing disposition of the accounts in the event of a divorce and the effect on elderly unmarried divorcees. Also needing careful attention is the effect on elderly surviving spouses. The degree to which workers choose joint-and-survivor annuitization is very sensitive to the way choices are presented to them. The Panel thinks that protection of a lower-earning spouse is important, and if a system does not mandate considerable benefits for a surviving spouse, it should at least have a division of accounts between spouses in some form.

The Panel thinks retirees should not be able to take all of their retirement benefits as a lump sum. Annuitization (through either a defined-benefit system or mandated annuitization of at least part of accumulations) or restrictions on the rate of monthly withdrawal should be part of the system. The Panel thinks that any mandated annuities should be annuities indexed for inflation.

The Panel thinks that income redistribution to low income workers to increase their replacement rates is an important aspect of Social Security. If a combined system does not sufficiently preserve the redistributive characteristics of the program, it should include additional contributions to individual accounts of low earners.

Glossary

401(k) plan   A defined contribution plan which enables employees to save for retirement by contributing a portion of their compensation on a pre-tax basis.

accumulations   The funds in a retirement account.

advance funding (Social Security)   The funding policy that is intended to build and maintain funds in the Social Security system beyond those needed to achieve target contingency reserves under pay-as-you-go financing policies.

adverse selection   A term used in the insurance field to describe a phenomenon whereby those more likely to use or benefit from the insurance are more likely to purchase it. For example, there is adverse selection when individuals voluntarily purchase annuities that guarantee monthly payments for as long as they live, because those with long life expectancy are more likely to buy them than those with short life expectancy. The selection is adverse to the insurer, in that long life expectancy would cost more than average life expectancy would indicate. By analogy, the concept extends to government programs with individual choice.

AFP (administradoras de fondos de pensiones)   In Chile, the private mutual funds set up to hold Chile's privatized social security individual accounts.

annuitization (life)   The process of converting the funds in a person's retirement account into monthly (or other periodic) income that is paid for the rest of the person's life; the purchase of an annuity.

annuity (life)   A guaranteed periodic (e.g. monthly, annual) income that is paid for the life of the annuity holder. Annuity contracts are sold by insurance companies. The insurance company receives premiums, either in a lump sum or a series of payments, from an annuity buyer and, in return, has a contractual obligation to pay a guaranteed income to the annuitant for the rest of his or her life.

basis point   One one-hundredth of a percent. One percentage point equals 100 basis points.

benefit formula (Social Security)   The formula used to calculate Social Security benefits. For retired workers, the basic benefit is based on their average indexed monthly earnings (AIME) over their highest 35 years of indexed earnings. For persons reaching age 62 in 1998, the formula is   90% of the first $477 of AIME, plus 32% of the next $2,398, plus 15% of AIME over $2,875. The basic benefit is reduced if claimed before normal retirement age (currently age 65), and is increased if retirement is delayed beyond the normal retirement age.

certificates of deposit (CDs)   A deposit at a bank or savings and loan institution which receives a stated interest rate and is available for withdrawal without penalty at a stated date.

charges   The fees charged by financial institutions to account holders. They may include management fees, which are paid to investment advisors who select and transact the investments. They also include charges to cover the cost of record keeping and other administrative functions. Some charges are made on deposits, some on withdrawals, and some annually on balances within an account. In some cases, the charges may be indirect—not explicitly separated from the interest rate paid on the deposit.

contingency reserve (Social Security)   In a pay-as-you-go Social Security system that lacks borrowing authority, a contingency reserve is a target amount of funds to be held in the Trust Funds to ensure that benefits can be paid during temporary or cyclic economic downturns. Past studies have recommended a target contingency reserve equal to about one year's benefit outgo.

contributions   Payments into a retirement plan. FICA taxes (see below) on earnings, or payroll taxes, are also called contributions.

corporate bond   An IOU issued by a corporation. By selling the bond, the corporation borrows money from the investors who purchase the bonds. Corporate bonds are also referred to as corporate debt instruments. Most bonds pay interest at regular intervals until they mature, at which point investors get their principal back. Alternatively, some bonds are sold at a discount to their face value—for example, $800 for a $1,000 bond—and do not pay interest at regular intervals. In this case, the investor gets $1,000 when the bond matures, receiving both the interest and principal repayment as a lump sum.

defined-benefit plan   A pension or retirement income plan which promises to pay retirement income to participants in an amount determined under a formula specified in the plan. Typically, the benefit formula is based on the participant's past earnings and duration of service in the plan. The plan sponsor is responsible for having sufficient funds to pay the promised benefits. The Social Security program is an example of a defined-benefit plan.

defined-contribution plan   A pension or retirement income plan in which contributions to participants' accounts determine the benefits paid to participants. Benefits paid from the plan are determined solely by the amount in a participant's account—that is, total past contributions, plus investment gains, minus investment losses and minus administrative expenses that are charged to plan participants.

diversification, diversified portfolio   An investment plan for an individual (or an entity such as a pension fund) that includes a mix of assets, that may include stocks, corporate bonds, and U.S. Treasury bonds. An investment portfolio holding stocks in many corporations is more diversified than one holding stocks in one or only a few corporations.

ERISA   The Employee Retirement Income Security Act of 1974, which sets forth comprehensive standards for private pension plans and other employee benefits.

federal budget, unified (surplus or deficit)   The total of all federal budget receipts minus the total of all outgo in a given year, including the two functions that are by law "off-budget": Social Security and the postal service. The portion of the budget that excludes the two "off-budget" functions is called the "on-budget" portion.

federal government debt   The federal debt is the total of all the Treasury bonds, bills and notes representing obligations of the federal government to repay the holders of these instruments. These bonds, bills and notes are held by the public and by various federal trust funds, including the Social Security Trust Fund. The debt is the net accumulation of past annual federal budget deficits and surpluses.

FICA   Federal Insurance Contributions Act, which authorizes collection of contributions (taxes) from employees and employers for the Social Security program and for Hospital Insurance under Medicare. The counterpart to FICA for the self-employed is the Self-Employment Contributions Act (SECA). "FICA" is sometimes used as shorthand to describe the taxes used to finance Social Security.

fiduciary   (1) Indicates a relationship of trust and confidence where one person (the fiduciary) holds or controls property for the benefit of another person; (2) anyone who exercises discretionary power and control, management, or disposition with regard to a fund's assets, or who has authority to do so, or who has discretionary authority or responsibility in the plan's administration.

fiduciary duty   Under ERISA, fiduciaries must discharge their duties solely in the interest of plan participants and their beneficiaries, and are accountable for any actions which may be construed by the courts as breaching that trust.

front-load   A form of charge that is collected when funds are deposited in an account.

funded, fully funded   A pension or retirement plan that holds sufficient funds today to finance all future benefits accrued as of today. For a defined-benefit plan, the degree of funding of the plan depends on projections of its future obligations and investment returns.

general revenues   Federal government revenues from general taxation, including federal personal and corporate income taxes. Excludes revenues (such as FICA taxes) that are earmarked for particular trust funds.

government-organized accounts   As used in this report, denotes individual-account systems in which the government arranges for both the record keeping for accounts and the investment management for the funds in the accounts—whether these functions are performed by government agencies or by private firms under contract to the government. The Thrift Savings Plan for federal employees is an example of government-organized accounts.

guaranteed products   A financial obligation by a financial institution that promises to pay a stated rate of return. Examples are stable value funds and certificates of deposit.

implicit rate of return, average (Social Security)   The interest rate (or discount rate) which equates the present value of contributions to the present value of benefits under Social Security. Rates of return are usually calculated for age groups, where probabilities of survival are averaged across all individuals in that age group.

index fund   A mutual fund that buys the stocks or bonds that make up a widely used market index, such as the Standard & Poor's 500. The goal of an index fund is to mirror market performance.

investment index   A calculation of the return from holding some given investment portfolio. One index widely used for stock market performance is the Standard & Poor's 500 Index, which measures the average performance of the stocks of the 500 largest corporations. Other indices are the Dow-Jones, Russell 3000, and the Wiltshire 5000.

Individual Retirement Account (IRA)   A personal, tax-deferred retirement account authorized under the Internal Revenue Code. Workers can hold a variety of financial investments in their IRAs, and IRAs can be provided by a variety of financial services institutions.

joint and survivor annuity   A guaranteed periodic income that is paid for the life of the annuity holder and his or her spouse (or other designated beneficiary). Joint-and-survivor annuity options vary in the proportions they pay to the survivor vis a vis the couple. The annuity that is paid while both beneficiaries are alive is less than would be paid if there were no survivor annuity.

lump-sum distribution (lump-sum withdrawals)   A single payment representing an individual's benefit held in a retirement plan. This is in contrast to having the entire amount paid out in monthly installments.

managed funds, managed portfolios   As distinct from index funds, managed funds use investment advisors to select stocks, bonds and other instruments in which to invest. Managed funds vary in their investment strategies.

money market fund   A mutual fund that invests in short-term IOUs of the government and highly rated corporations. Money market funds pay a fluctuating interest rate, but maintain a fixed dollar per share value.

money's worth   Any measure of the value of benefits in relation to the taxes or contributions for the benefits, for example, the average implicit rate of return an age cohort of workers can expect to receive on their lifetime contributions to Social Security.

mutual fund   An investment company that pools the money of many individual investors and uses it to buy stocks, bonds, money market instruments, and other assets.

national capital   The aggregate amount of capital available for production in a year. Capital includes business plant and equipment, and housing.

national income   The total income received in the economy in a given year, which includes wages and profits.

national savings The portion of national income in a given year that is not consumed. National savings is made up of three parts: government savings (or dissavings); corporate savings; and personal (or household) savings.

nominal annuities Annuities that have payments that are stated in dollar terms, for example, the same amount each month. An increasing nominal annuity is one that increases by a fixed percentage each year. This is in contrast with real annuities, that are indexed to keep pace with inflation.

non-Social Security budget The unified federal budget minus the operations (income and outgo) of the Social Security program.

non-Social Security surplus or deficit The annual balance in the unified federal budget after subtracting the operations of the Social Security program.

OASI Old-Age and Survivors Insurance (the monthly benefits paid to retired workers and dependents and survivors of insured workers by Social Security and the financing for those benefits).

OASDI Old-Age and Survivors Insurance and Disability Insurance (the monthly benefits paid to retired workers, disabled workers, and dependents and survivors of insured workers by Social Security and the financing for those benefits).

pay-as-you-go (Social Security) Social Security financing policies in which current revenues to the system are set to be sufficient to pay current benefits and administrative costs, while maintaining a target contingency reserve.

payroll tax A tax on earnings of workers. As used in this report, "payroll tax" refers to the taxes on earnings that are used to pay for the Social Security program, and excludes the payroll tax that supports Medicare Hospital Insurance. The Social Security tax is currently 12.4 percent of earnings, or 6.2 percent paid by employees and employers each, up to a maximum taxable earnings amount that is $68,400 in 1998.

present value, present discounted value The amount of current dollars which would grow at an appropriate interest rate to equal a given number of dollars at some date in the future.

portfolio   A set of financial investments held by an investor.

privately organized accounts   In this report, denotes individual account systems in which individuals directly select private firms to do the record keeping and investment management. IRAs are examples of privately organized accounts.

real annuities, inflation-indexed annuities, indexed annuities
Annuities that are automatically adjusted to keep pace with inflation.

real wage growth   Wage growth in excess of price inflation.

risk premium   The difference between an expected return on an asset and the return available from a safe asset of the same maturity.

SERPS (State Earnings-Related Pension System)   The earnings-related portion of the British public pension system.

single-life annuity   A guaranteed periodic income that is paid for the life of one individual (as distinct from joint-and-survivor annuity).

social investing   An investment strategy that is influenced by social or policy goals other than simply balancing risk and return for investors.

SSI   Supplemental Security Income program, a federal program to provide monthly cash benefits to aged, blind and disabled persons with very low incomes and resources. In 1998, the maximum federal SSI benefit is $494 per month for an individual, $741 for a couple.

stable value funds   A type of conservative investment fund that invests in medium-term fixed income investment contracts which offer the investor the ability to withdraw or transfer funds without any market value risk (risk of principal loss as interest rates rise) or other penalty for premature withdrawal. The issuer of the investment contracts—a high quality investment institution—guarantees principal plus accumulated interest and an interest rate for a specified period of time.

stock   An ownership share in a corporation; also called an "equity." Some stocks pay periodic dividends (a share of the company's profits) to their owners. When selling a stock, it may be sold at a higher or lower price than was originally paid.

Thrift Savings Plan (TSP)   The 401(k) type of plan that was enacted in 1984 for federal employees.

Treasury bond   An IOU issued by the federal government; also called "debt." By selling a bond, the federal government borrows money from the investor who purchases it and has a legal contract to pay it back with interest. Treasury also sells short-term debt, called "notes" and "bills."

Trust Fund (Social Security)   The Social Security program—Old-Age, Survivors and Disability Insurance (OASDI)—has Trust Funds that receive revenue earmarked for this program and from which benefits and administrative expenses are paid. There are separate trust funds for Old-Age and Survivors Insurance (OASI) and for Disability Insurance (DI). In this report, "Trust Fund" refers to the combined OASDI Trust Funds.

Trust Fund actuarial balance (Social Security)   The difference (on a present-value basis) over the 75-year long-range projection period used by the Social Security Trustees between expected income (from payroll taxes, from the income taxation of Social Security benefits, and including the balance at the start of the period) and expected cost (benefit payments, administrative costs, and including the cost of attaining and maintaining a specified target contingency reserve.) It is expressed as a percentage of wages that are taxable for Social Security. The 1998 Trustees' Report projected an actuarial deficit of 2.19 percent of taxable payroll.

Trust Fund actuarial deficit   A negative actuarial balance; revenues are less than expenditures.

Trust Fund surplus (Social Security)   Excess of revenues over expenditures in a given year.

unfunded obligations of Social Security   The unfunded obligation (called the "unfunded liability") can be calculated three different ways.

The concept used for assessing the financial status of a Social

Security program intended to be financed on a pay-as-you-go basis, the "open group" definition, is equal to all the benefits expected to be paid out over a defined period (say, the next 75 years), including the benefits not yet earned, minus the current value of the trust fund and of all revenues expected over the same period, including payroll taxes of people not yet in the workforce. This is a present value measure of the actuarial imbalance, and is estimated to be about $2.9 trillion for OASDI (Goss, forthcoming). This measure roughly matches the actuarial imbalance of 2.19 percent of taxable payroll.

The appropriate concept for evaluating the cost of a transition to a program intended to be fully advance funded (called the "plan-termination unfunded accrued liability" in the context of such plans), is equal to the present value of benefits (net of income taxes paid on these benefits that are directed to OASDI) earned to date by current workers and beneficiaries minus the current value of the trust fund. No future expected payroll tax revenues (even from those now in the workforce) are included.

For a transition to a program intended to be fully advance funded, this value may be referred to as "maximum transition cost." This is estimated to be about $9 trillion (Goss, forthcoming).

A third concept is the "closed group" definition, equal to all of the benefits which have been earned to date, plus those expected to be earned in the future, by persons already in the workforce, minus income taxes paid on those benefits that are directed to OASDI, minus the trust fund and minus the expected future payroll taxes of those who are already in the workforce. That is, this definition excludes future taxes and benefits of those not yet in the workforce. The concept provides an alternative measure of "plan termination liability" for transition to a fully advance funded program for future generations. This value provides a rough measure of the intergenerational transfer expected from future entrants into the workforce to those who have already entered the workforce. It is currently estimated to be about $9 trillion (Goss, forthcoming).

Notes

1. A dissenting view holds that the relative magnitude of TSP equity holdings versus the potential holdings by the Social Security Trust Fund are so different that the comparison drawn here is inappropriate.

2. Dallas Salisbury does not think that an individual account system for over 140 million workers is feasible at acceptable administrative cost in the absence of new technological developments.

3. A dissenting view is that a Social Security Trust Fund sponsored by the federal government should not manage the potential large accumulation of funds for the same reasons discussed above.

4. A dissenting view is that wider latitude of investment choices should be considered on investments above some minimum standard.

5. Some analysts disagree with this conclusion, but recognize the importance of properly accounting for potential adverse selection if voluntary opt-out were allowed.

6. A dissenting view prefers the alternative approach to improving the net market return for small accounts of providing a governmental "match" for low earners.

7. A dissenting view prefers to have privately organized accounts from the beginning.

8. Since forecasting all the factors—real wage growth, mortality and fertility trends—that will determine outlays and revenues into the distant future is difficult, the Trustees provide alternative scenarios, labeled low cost and high cost, to provide some sense of the uncertainty of the projections.

9. There are separate trust funds for Old-Age and Survivors Insurance

and Disability Insurance. For our purposes, there is no need to distinguish between them and we refer to the combined Trust Funds when we discuss the Trust Fund.

10. See Geanakoplos, Mitchell, and Zeldes (1998a and 1998b) for further discussion.

11. Currently, Social Security has "individual accounts" in the sense that records are kept of individual earnings histories and benefits are based on those earnings histories. Thus, Social Security is a "defined benefit" system in that benefits are given by law as a function of the history of covered earnings. We will use the term individual accounts to refer to funded, defined-contribution individual accounts, not individual earnings histories. With a "defined contribution" system, benefits equal the level that can be financed from the accumulation in an individual account. It is the level of contributions, not the formula for benefits that is legislated. We will not consider individual defined contribution accounts that are not funded, sometimes referred to as "notional accounts."

12. Tax revenues include FICA payments by employers, employees and the self-employed and a portion of the income tax revenue from the taxation of Social Security benefits that is allocated to Social Security. Tax revenue can be changed by changing the payroll tax rate, changing the maximum taxable earnings level, or changing the income tax treatment of benefits. Mandating payments into individual accounts is another way of increasing the flow of revenues into a reformed Social Security. Changing the coverage of Social Security, by including workers not currently covered by Social Security also increases tax revenues and, eventually, benefits. Changing the growth of the economy will also change tax revenues, and eventually benefits.

13. While expenditures include both benefits paid and the administrative expenses of running Social Security, the latter are a very small part of annual expenditures (less than 1 percent) and are not considered.

14. We do not draw the important distinction between government investment and other government expenditures.

15. For discussion of issues in corporate responses to Social Security reform, see "The Vital Connection: An Analysis of the Impact of Social Security Reform On Employer-Sponsored Retirement Plans" by ERISA Industry Committee.

16. A recommendation by the Panel is not necessarily unanimous, but has the support of at least 3/4 of the members of the Panel.

17. A dissenting view is that this is an impossible scenario, i.e. that it is

unlikely that a multi-trillion dollar Trust Fund could be sustained without spending the surplus in some manner.

18. Treasury bonds are not riskless since their real value depends on the history of inflation. Interest rate changes also change the value of a bond. The special issue bonds held by the Trust Fund can be redeemed at par, but historically this option has only been used when the Trust Fund has been forced to sell bonds.

19. According to the 1995 Survey of Consumer Finances, 49 percent of households headed by persons aged 21–62 have financial assets (including defined contribution pensions) of less than $10,000 (tabulation by John Ameriks and Stephen Zeldes).

20. A dissenting view is that there are policy considerations overriding the risk-return discussion in these sections. In this view, the optimal portfolio for a Social Security Trust Fund should continue to be 100 percent government bonds. The analysis solely in terms of risk and return suggests that the system could remain funded and would not be subject to political manipulation in the future, a conclusion that is not appropriate in this view.

21. John Geanakoplos and Stephen Zeldes are concerned about the way the political process would make use of estimates of actuarial balance. The intermediate cost estimate is not designed or intended to account or adjust for risk. Shifting the Trust Fund into equities would both improve the measured actuarial balance and increase the risk of the system. Geanakoplos and Zeldes are concerned that the political process would put too much weight on the improvement in measured actuarial balance, and too little weight on the added risk. The same concern arises with individual accounts investing in equities, if cuts in benefits in the defined benefit portion are tied explicitly to returns on individual accounts. Even if benefits are not explicitly tied to individual account returns, a similar issue may arise if the political decision about benefit cuts overemphasizes the increased expected return and underemphasizes the added risk, from investing in equities in individual accounts.

22. Other measures of money's worth are the expected net present value of taxes and benefits and the expected present value of benefits divided by the expected present value of taxes. See, e.g. Advisory Council on Social Security, 1996.

23. The size of the gain from such intergenerational risk-sharing would be smaller in the presence of other government policies that provide similar risk-sharing. In particular, through both the corporate and personal income taxes, federal revenue shares in the return to risky investment.

This variation in revenue affects tax and spending policy over time and so is a form of risk-sharing that is partially intergenerational . However, other programs (other than Medicare) do not have the same age structure as Social Security and so cannot produce precisely the same pattern.

24. John Geanakoplos and Stephen Zeldes also worry that a relative over-attention to the improved actuarial balance and a relative underattention to the added risk of Trust Fund investment in equities might sidetrack or delay other reforms to improve Social Security. A similar concern arises regarding equity investment in individual accounts.

25. John Geanakoplos thinks that consideration should be given to putting a cap on Trust Fund ownership of corporate bonds as well.

26. A dissenting view is that the relative magnitude of TSP equity holdings versus the potential holdings by the Social Security Trust Fund are so different that the comparison drawn here is inappropriate.

27. Hammond and Warshawsky (1997) estimated that by 2020 the Advisory Council's individual account plan would hold 1 to 3 percent of the market and the plan for central trust fund investment would hold 2 to 5 percent of the market, assuming 9 percent and 5 percent growth rates for the market. In contrast, if the market fell by 2 percent per year, the fractions held would be 17 percent and 28 percent.

28. Dallas Salisbury does not think than an individual account system for over 140 million workers, with less than an 18 to 24 month lag in account recording, is feasible at acceptable administrative cost in the absence of new technological developments, including moving 5.5 million small employers from paper filing to automated filing.

29. For more discussion of implementation tasks, see Reno, 1998.

30. A dissenting view notes that the Social Security Board, the precedent organization to the Social Security Administration, set up a system to record personal earnings records on 26 million workers in less than 16 months after the passage of the Social Security Act in August 1935, in an era prior to the availability of electronic computers, and electronic data storage and retrieval systems.

31. Dallas Salisbury does not agree that what was done in the beginning of Social Security is relevant to the challenge of implementation of individual accounts. The differences between a wage credit system and a cash credit system are substantial. Once investment options are introduced the complexity of administration is magnified, not to speak of the need for education. There is lots of time to correct bad records in a wage credit system. A cash plan like TSP requires detailed records and communication, and errors are something that the participant sees quickly.

32. Statistical Supplement to the Social Security Bulletin, 1998, p. 163, 167 and 197.

33. The estimate for TSP is based on its 1997 balance sheet and includes: administrative costs of $44.1 million; investment management fees of $2.3 million; and fiduciary insurance of $0.2 million, divided by 2.3 million participants (Arthur Anderson LLP, 1998).

34. A dissenting view is the estimated marginal resources needed to administer the hypothetical system presented here are significantly exaggerated. Social Security is already collecting sufficient information to allocate payroll tax collections to workers' individual accounts. Instead of posting annual earnings, the administrative staff can post a contribution as a percentage of annual earnings and allocate the tax revenues accordingly.

35. A review of staffing levels by defined contribution administrators in the private sector suggests ratios of over 1.0 per 1000 participants. Dallas Salisbury estimates this would mean staffing for the new system of over 100,000 workers, under very conservative assumptions assuming substantial economies of scale. An individual accounts system with SSA administration and annual W-2 contributions would likely require lower staffing.

36. Similar risk issues are present without annuitizaiton.

37. As described earlier, the size of the gain from such intergenerational risk-sharing would be smaller in the presence of other government policies that provide similar risk-sharing.

38. For analysis of portfolio choice by TIAA-CREF participants, see Ameriks and Zeldes, 1998.

39. Yuan Chang believes individual accounts implies private ownership, so it is inevitable that some heirs will receive benefits from such accounts at the death of retirees. These benefits represent a leakage of system resources. The existence of such benefits must be considered extraneous and would be inconsistent, at least in appearance, with the concept of the Social Security system being a social safety net.

40. Yuan Chang believes demographics affect system financing in three different ways, two of which present a problem only under pay-as-you-go financing. One is the imbalance between benefits and contributions due primarily to the cyclicality of birth rates. Secular trends toward lower birth rates coupled with increasing longevity creates the dependency ratio problem, which would not by itself require changes in benefits or contributions if the system were accurately funded.

The third is that increasing longevity implies that the same benefit contribution formula does not hold for each new group that enters the employment market. This is true even if the system were fully funded. There is a built in increase in deficit if the same benefit-contribution relationship is held over a long period of time. I agree that the rising dependency ratio could be taken care of with rising productivity and thus rising real wages. But there are not mechanics that address the creeping deficit built into the constancy of the benefit-contribution formula. Deficits will automatically widen, albeit by a small amount each year. That is why we are still projecting deficits beyond 75 years; and we always will so long as we assume that mortality will continue to improve with no end in sight.

In keeping with the requirement that benefits must equal contributions over a long period of time, the most permanent solution for a defined benefit is to build in an automatic increase in the retirement age for each generation of new workers. Certain limited adjustments have already been separately legislated. It is also an element in the recent reform in Sweden. For individual accounts, the solution would have to be a continuously increasing contribution.

41. For example, disabled workers might get access to the funds in their individual accounts when they reach retirement age. Some workers with similar earnings histories will have different amounts in their accounts. Thus it is impossible to have a formula where the level of monthly disability benefits adjusts to just match the value of access to retirement funds for all workers. This unevenness in resources may be a problem for some workers. For more discussion of the integration issue, see Diamond, Goss, and Reno, 1998.

42. See, e.g., U.S. Department of Health, Education, and Welfare (1979), U.S. House of Representatives, Committee on Ways and Means (1985), U.S. Congressional Budget Office (1986), and U.S. House of Representatives, Select Committee on Aging (1992).

43. With annual adjustments, the same people would be taxed in some years and subsidized in others, increasing distortions. With lifetime adjustments, individuals would not know their implicit tax rates since the rates would be dependent on future labor market experiences. In this way lifetime adjustments are similar in their effects to the use of a progressive defined benefit formula.

44. Stephen Zeldes thinks that insufficient attention has been paid in this section of the report to two features of the current system. First, while there are many beneficial risk-sharing properties of the redistribution in the current system, some of the redistribution is arbitrary and not based on sound economic principles. Second, the current system has certain features that make it complicated for households to understand what their future benefits are likely to be and what factors the benefits will depend

on. Although these features could be improved within the current defined-benefit system, such improvements might be easier to implement in the context of a shift to an individual account system.

45. Peter Diamond agrees that it is complicated for households to understand the determinants of benefits under the current system. But it is also complicated for households to understand the retirement incomes they would have with individual accounts. The first complication is that the accumulation in an account depends on rates of return in the future. Even knowing future contributions, a worker can not know the accumulation at retirement, only a stochastic distribution of possible accumulations, a distribution that differs with different models of the stochastic structure of future rates of return. Second, many workers do not have a good picture of the level of annuity that could be purchased with a given accumulation, or, alternatively, the level of consumption that could be financed in retirement without undue risk of outliving available resources.

46. A dissenting view is that history may shed some light on the prospect of greater funding being realized. The funding provisions under the original Social Security Act and Amendments adopted in 1939 and several times throughout the 1940s were not achieved. In each case, the funding provisions were cut back by reducing scheduled payroll tax rates, by increasing benefits, or both. They also note that the projected funding under the 1983 Amendments did not lead to added national savings because the increase in the trust fund balances were used to finance other government consumption expenditures.

47. Peter Diamond disagrees with the analyses in the preceding note. Political history from the 1930s and 1940s can shed very little light on the prospect of greater funding being realized. In the earlier period, Social Security was small and new, the system was immature in its extent and history of coverage, and we were in the Great Depression, in World War II, and then in a postwar period with great uncertainty about economic prospects. Circumstances have changed so much as to make that history of very limited relevance for predictive purposes.

In addition, he disagrees with the analysis of the effect of the 1983 amendments on national savings. Analysis of the impact on the non-Social Security budget requires consideration of what would have happened if the Social Security legislation had been different. There is no way to know that for sure. The range of possibilities is wide since the federal government would have had no difficulty borrowing from other sources if Social Security were not purchasing Treasury bonds. Merely pointing out that there was a deficit and that the Trust Fund holds Treasury bonds can not lead to any conclusion about the contribution to national savings.

The budget deficits throughout the 1980s were a large problem that Congress found difficult to address. Subtracting Social Security surpluses, the commonly reported unified budget deficits would have been larger, e.g., $205 billion in 1989, rather than $153 billion. Somewhat higher deficits might have led to larger tax increases or expenditure cuts. On the other hand, they might not have led to significantly different legislation, as seems most plausible to me given the difficulty experienced in legislating tax increases and spending cuts, both politically unpopular. Indeed, the Social Security surplus was larger in 1990 and 1993 when we did significantly raise taxes than earlier, when we did not.

One can reasonably argue that once legislation started moving toward "budget balance in 2002," the Social Security surplus might have lowered the non-Social Security deficit. Without the Social Security surplus, the target of "budget balance in 2002" might well have seemed politically infeasible and there might not have been a drive for budget balance for that year. While some other target might have been chosen, that might have resulted in a larger deficit.

The argument in the previous note suggests that without the Social Security surplus, Congress would have legislated decreases in government consumption expenditures equal to the surplus. I find far more plausible the hypothesis that expenditure cuts beyond the levels that were legislated were so difficult that the deficit in the non-Social Security budget would have been roughly the same if Social Security were in balance. With this hypothesis, the surplus was roughly all saved and did add to national savings, although it is difficult to say exactly how much.

48. A dissenting view holds that a trust fund sponsored by the federal government should not manage the potential large accumulation of funds for the same reasons stated in Section 2-5.

49. A dissenting view holds that wider latitude of choices should be considered on investments above some minimum standard.

50. There is a sizable market for "individual annuities" which are savings vehicles which include an annuity option, but do not contain a commitment to receiving the accumulation as an annuity. Overwhelming, these policies do not appear to be taken as annuitized benefits.

51. A dissenting view disagrees with this conclusion, but recognizes the importance of properly accounting for potential adverse selection if voluntary opt-out were allowed.

52. A dissenting view holds that it is preferable to have privately organized accounts from the beginning.

References

Advisory Council on Social Security, 1996. *Report of the 1994–95 Advisory Council on Social Security.*

Ameriks, J., and Zeldes, S. P. (unpublished tabulations). 1995 Survey of Consumer Finances.

Ameriks, J., and Zeldes, S. P. 1998. "Portfolio Choice in Retirement Accounts: An Analysis of Longitudinal Data from TIAA-CREF," manuscript, Columbia University.

Arnold, R. D. 1998. "The Political Feasibility of Social Security Reform." *Framing the Social Security Debate: Values, Politics, and Economics,* R. D. Arnold, M. J. Graetz, and A. H. Munnell (eds), Washington, D.C.: National Academy of Social Insurance.

Arthur Andersen LLP. 1998. "Financial Statements of the Thrift Savings Fund—1997 and 1998."

Bayer, P., Bernheim, B. D., and Scholz, J. 1996. "The Effects of Financial Education in the Workplace: Evidence from a Survey of Employers," National Bureau of Economic Research Working Paper.

Board of Trustees, Federal Old-Age and Survivors Insurance and Disability Insurance Trust Funds. 1998. *1998 Annual Report.* Washington, D.C.: U.S. Government Printing Office.

Bohn, H. 1997. "Social Security Reform and Financial Markets." *Social Security Reform: Links to Saving, Investment and Growth,* S. A. Sass and R. K. Triest (eds), Federal Reserve Bank of Boston, Conference Series No. 41.

Boskin, M. 1998. "Background for the Social Security Reform Debate." *Framing the Social Security Debate: Values, Politics, and Economics,* R. D. Arnold, M. J. Graetz, and A. H. Munnell (eds), Washington, D.C.: National Academy of Social Insurance.

Bosworth, B. and Burtless, G. 1997. "Social Security Reform in a Global Context." *Social Security Reform: Links to Saving, Investment and Growth,* S. A. Sass and R. K. Triest (eds), Federal Reserve Bank of Boston, Conference Series No. 41.

Coile, C., and Diamond, P. 1998. "Changes in Income and Assets in the NBDS by Marital Status." Mimeo, MIT.

Daniel, C. "Taxing Reforms for British Retirees," *Washington Post,* August 9, 1998, section C–3.

Diamond, P. 1992. "Organizing the Health Insurance Market." *Econometrica,* 60: 1233–1254.

Diamond, P., Goss, S., and Reno., V. 1998. "Shifting from DB to DC Benefits: Implications for Workers' Disability and Young Survivor Benefits," Working Paper prepared for the Panel on Privatization of Social Security. National Academy of Social Insurance (www. nasi. org).

Diamond, P. 1998. "Economics of Social Security Reform." *Framing the Social Security Debate: Values, Politics, and Economics,* R. D. Arnold, M. J. Graetz, and A. H. Munnell (eds), Washington, D.C.: National Academy of Social Insurance.

Employee Benefit Research Institute. 1997. *EBRI Databook on Employee Benefits,* 4th edition. Washington, D.C.: Employee Benefit Research Institute.

Employee Benefit Research Institute. 1994. "Employment-Based Retirement Income Benefits: Analysis of the April 1993 Current Population Survey." *EBRI Special Report SR–25/Issue Brief* no. 153.

ERISA Industry Committee. 1998. *The Vital Connection: An Analysis of the Impact of Social Security Reform On Employer-Sponsored Retirement Plans.* Washington, D.C.: ERISA Industry Committee.

Geanakoplos, J., Mitchell, O., and Zeldes, S. 1998a. "Social Security Money's Worth." *National Bureau of Economic Research Working Paper,* No. 6722, September 1998.

Geanakoplos, J. Mitchell, O., and Zeldes, S. 1998b. "Would a Privatized Social Security System Really Pay a Higher Rate of Return?" *Framing the Social Security Debate: Values, Politics, and Economics,* R. D. Arnold, M. J. Graetz, and A. H. Munnell (eds), Washington, D.C.: National Academy of Social Insurance.

Goodfellow, G., and Schieber, S. (forthcoming.) "Simulating Benefit Levels Under Alternative Social Security Reform Approaches." *Prospects for Social Security Reform,* O. Mitchell, R. Myers, and H. Young (eds), Philadelphia, PA: University of Pennsylvania Press.

Goss, S. (forthcoming.) "Measuring Solvency in the Social Security System." *Prospects for Social Security Reform,* O. Mitchell, R. Myers, and H. Young (eds), Philadelphia, PA: University of Pennsylvania Press.

Grad, S. 1998. *Income of the Population 55 or Older,* 1996. Washington, D.C.: U.S. Social Security Administration, Office of Research, Evaluation and Statistics.

Hammond, B., and Warshawsky, M. 1997. "Investing Social Security Funds in Stocks." *Benefits Quarterly,* 13 (3) 52–86.

Heclo, H. 1998. "A Political Science Perspective on Social Security Reform." *Framing the Social Security Debate: Values, Politics, and Economics,* R. D. Arnold, M. J. Graetz, and A. H. Munnell (eds), Washington, D.C.: National Academy of Social Insurance.

Holden, K. 1998. "Insuring Against the Consequences of Widowhood in a Reformed Social Security System." Framing the Social Security Debate: Values, Politics, and Economics, R. D. Arnold, M. J. Graetz, and A. H. Munnell (eds), Washington, D.C.: National Academy of Social Insurance.

Mitchell, O., and Moore, J. (forthcoming.) "Retirement Wealth Accumulation and Decumulation: New Developments and Outstanding Opportunities." *Journal of Risk and Insurance.*

Mitchell, O., Poterba, J., Warshawsky, M., and Brown, J. (forthcoming.) "New Evidence on the Money's Worth of Individual Annuities." *American Economic Review.*

Olsen, K., VanDerhei, J., Salisbury, D., and Holmer, M. 1998. "How Do Individual Social Security Accounts Stack Up? An Evaluation Using the EBRI-SSASIM2 Policy Simulation Model." *EBRI Issue Brief* no. 195. Washington, D.C.: Employee Benefit Research Institute.

Perun, P. 1998. "Defined Contribution Accounts Under Social Security: Their Implications for Distribution." Working Paper prepared for the Panel on Privatization of Social Security. (Also available at www. planetnow.com.)

Perun, P. 1998. "Designing the Investment Program for Defined Contribution Accounts Under Social Security." Working Paper prepared for the Panel on Privatization of Social Security. (Also available at www. planetnow. com.)

Social Security Administration. 1997. *Annual Statistical Supplement to the Social Security Bulletin.* Washington, D.C.: Social Security Administration, Office of Research, Evaluation and Statistics.

Shoven, J. and Wise, D. 1998. "The Taxation of Pensions: A Shelter Can Become a Trap." *Frontiers in the Economics of Aging,* D. A. Wise (ed), University of Chicago Press, 173–211.

U.S. Congressional Budget Office. 1986. *Earnings Sharing Options for the Social Security System.*

U.S. Department of Health, Education, and Welfare. 1979. *Social Security and the Changing Roles of Men and Women.*

U.S. House of Representatives. Committee on Ways and Means. 1985. Report on Earnings Sharing Implementation Study. WMCP 99–4. 99th Congress. Washington, D.C.: U.S. Government Printing Office.

U.S. House of Representatives. Select Committee on Aging. 1992. Congressional Symposium on Women and Retirement. Hearing, Comm. Pub. 102–897. 102nd Congress. Washington, D.C.: U.S. Government Printing Office.

Yakobowski, P., and Reilly, A. 1994. "Salary Reduction Plan and Individual Saving for Retirement." *EBRI Issue Brief* no. 155. Washington. D.C.: Employee Benefit Research Institute.

Appendix A: Statement of Qualification of Participation of Stephen C. Goss

November 17, 1998

The analysis of a wide range of issues included in this report should be of great value to all persons engaged in developing or evaluating proposals for reforming the Social Security program. It has been a privilege to serve as a member of the panel.

However, the report also includes recommendations and statements of belief about a number of specific options related to Social Security reform. In my capacity as the Deputy Chief Actuary for Long-Range Projections for the Social Security Administration, I must evaluate the financial effects of all proposals being considered for Social Security reform. It is inappropriate for me to make personal judgements on many of the options raised in the report. For this reason my position is to abstain from voting on all of the recommendations and statements of belief in this report.

Stephen C. Goss
Deputy Chief Actuary

Long-Range Actuarial Estimates
Social Security Administration

Appendix B

MEMORANDUM

TO: NASI Social Security Reform Panel Members

FROM: Michael J. Boskin
             Olivia S. Mitchell
             Sylvester J. Schieber

SUBJECT: Our Resignation from the NASI Panel

DATE: October 14, 1998

We are writing to inform you that we have reluctantly come to the decision to resign from the NASI Social Security Reform Panel on which we have worked together for the past two years. We also want to explain why we have reached this conclusion.

Over the last several iterations of the draft report, we have repeatedly expressed our concerns about the general tone of the report and about specific matters of content. Although we each commented on most of the drafts of the report, we have not been wholly satisfied with the responses to our comments. Several of the matters that we have raised individually, we continue to believe are important yet do not appear in the current version. For example, at a Panel meeting and in writing, Olivia raised a concern that the report did not take due account of the role of SSI in considering alternative reform options. She believed that such a discussion would be included in the report, yet there is no proper discussion of this in the current version. Michael, Olivia, and Syl several times asked to have material included about the magnitude of the Social Security problem, yet this was not incorporated until the very last draft circulated to us (with no time remaining to discuss content). Syl raised questions repeatedly about the political risk discussion, questions that were not satisfactorily addressed. And finally, each of us had several times raised questions about the general lack of balance in the tone of the report.

In our view, the fact that the Panel stipulated that a 75 percent vote would be sufficient for a "Panel recommendation" led the us down the path that dissatisfied several panel members, and particularly the three of us. At the time this stipulation was discussed, we did not perceive that a 75 percent rule, compounded over many findings arranged in a particular order, would produce a "more than the sum of the parts" phenomenon deleterious to those with minority viewpoints. We have concluded that the 75 percent rule produced a report that can be read as overly strongly favoring the majority position. As one Panel member other than the three of us said, "Anyone reading the report will conclude that we favor a trust fund surplus partly invested in equities and individual accounts are too expensive." None of us supports that position, nor do we believe the substance remotely merits those conclusions. Perhaps a different approach, one that emphasized the many things we all agreed on, with separate minority/majority discussions recording our disagreements in more detail, would have been more acceptable.

We appreciate the considerable time pressure that Peter has been under, and the tremendous amount of work that he has done to bring the project along in the Panel's behalf. We have also each communicated to him in recent weeks that there was more work to be done, and that the time frame for releasing the report prior to the November elections was unrealistic.

At the end of last week, we were presented with a new draft of the report, and a tight time schedule intended to complete the work by Tuesday morning of this week. Meanwhile Michael had contracted the flu last week that added to his back problems. Olivia and Syl remained unsatisfied with the tone of the draft report and with a number of substantive issues raised on prior occasions. Late Monday afternoon, Olivia and Syl were offered the opportunity to draft a dissent to be included with the report. Both of them face demanding work schedules that make it impossible to develop a full-blown dissent under the Panel's scheduling constraint. A dissent that would address the range of tone and content concerns remaining would take considerable time, and it certainly could not have been completed in time to issue the report prior to the upcoming election day. Michael was also asked to draft a minority report or dissent, but decided it would both considerably delay and distract from the final report. He personally takes some of the responsibility for not being able to achieve mutually agreeable content within the specified timetable or to obtain agreement on a more reasonable timetable.

Our remaining disagreements are such that we cannot sign the report at this juncture, and hence we are each withdrawing from the Panel. Nevertheless we believe that the current version of the Panel report contains much worthwhile material, and we have benefited from participating in the Panel learning and discussion process. We wish the Panel well in the release of the report. We especially wish to thank each of you for your efforts. We have learned a great deal in the course of the Panel's work and sincerely appreciate the opportunity of working with you.

Best wishes.